Presented To:

_____

From:

_____

Date:

_____

SOUND WISDOM BOOKS BY JIM STOVALL

The Millionaire Map

WISDOM *for* WINNERS

A MILLIONAIRE MINDSET

JIM STOVALL

AN OFFICIAL PUBLICATION OF
THE NAPOLEON HILL FOUNDATION

Sound Wisdom

P.O. Box 310

Shippensburg, PA 17257-0310

International rights inquiries please contact The Napoleon Hill Foundation at 276-328-6700

email: napoleonhill@uvawise.edu

For more information on foreign distribution, call 717-530-2122.

Reach us on the Internet: www.soundwisdom.com.

ISBN 13 TP: 978-0-7684-0507-1

ISBN 13 Ebook: 978-0-7684-0508-8

For Worldwide Distribution, Printed in the U.S.A.

1 2 3 4 5 6 7 8 / 18 17 16 15 14

FOREWORD

WEBSTER'S NEW WORLD DICTIONARY **DESCRIBES WISDOM AS "THE** quality of being wise, good judgment." Succeeding in life can begin with something as simple as choosing a book, reading the book and applying the message. A tremendous place to start is with any of Jim Stovall's twenty books. Then apply the wisdom that Stovall shares as you read his books or articles.

Should you have any question as to the author's qualifications to impart wisdom, perhaps a little of his background will shed some light on the matter.

Proverbs 27:19 tell us, "we become like those with whom we associate: a mirror reflects a man's face, but what he is really like is shown by the kind of friends he chooses." Jim Stovall chose wisely, being mentored by Lee Braxton an associate of Napoleon Hill. It was Lee Braxton who delivered Hill's eulogy. Napoleon Hill and W. Clement Stone, in their best seller *Success through a Positive Mental Attitude,* wrote about Lee Braxton.

Braxton was born into poverty in a family of twelve children. Lee Braxton was a man of character, a religious man who believed that God is always a good God. Facing difficulties, he lost his job. His home was about to be taken and all seemed hopeless. Braxton prayed for guidance. As if an answer to his prayer, a friend gave him the book *Think and Grow Rich.*

His friend had lost his job and home during the Depression and was able to regain his fortune after reading *Think and Grow Rich.* Eventually, Braxton founded a bank and retired at age 44 to engage in a life of ministry. Being mentored by men like Lee Braxton as well as Jim Stovall's father who worked at Oral Robert's University for over fifty years contributed to the success of Stovall.

Jim Stovall is now a renowned author best known for his bestselling book *The Ultimate Gift* which was made into a movie starring James Garner and Abigail Breslin. A graduate of Oral Roberts University with an Honorary Doctorate of Law for his work with the disabled, Stovall is blind and has become a leading advocate for the blind by making television and movies available to blind people. His leadership as President of Narrative Television won the Emmy Award for its work. Steve Forbes, CEO of *Forbes* magazine says, "Jim Stovall is one of the most extraordinary men of our era."

The President's Committee of Equal Opportunity selected Jim as the Entrepreneur of the Year. Jim also has been named International Humanitarian of the Year joining President Jimmy Carter and Mother Teresa as recipients of this honor.

For several years, Jim Stovall has written a column with the worthy title *Winners' Wisdom*. What started as a simple request to do a short literary piece grew in popularity. The column became a regular piece from Stovall and has been read by literally millions whether in newspapers, magazines or today's popular social media such as emails and Facebook.

Through the generosity of Jim who is contributing his many years of work to be published in a book by the non-profit Napoleon Hill Foundation, whether you are reading one message or several at a time, you will appreciate the knowledge and inspiration contained on every page.

—**DON M. GREEN** is Executive Director of the nonprofit Napoleon Hill Foundation, a position he has held for fourteen years. Don is a board member of The University of Virginia/Wise and president of the University of Virginia/Wise Foundation Board. Prior to his position with the Napoleon Hill Foundation, he was a bank president for twenty years.

INTRODUCTION

THE JOURNEY THAT IS THIS LIFE CAN BE BEST REPRESENTED BY A winding, twisting back road with many delays and detours. As we are going through any phase of life, it can seem like we are confronted with utter chaos, but when, from time to time, we reach a milestone or arrive at a mountain peak and look back along our route, we can often observe a divine order that was not apparent as we traveled.

As an author who writes books I can't read that are made into movies I can't see, I find it ironic that, as a blind person myself, I became an internationally-syndicated columnist. After my first book entitled *You Don't Have To Be Blind To See* hit the bookstores almost 20 years ago and began finding a bit of success, I was contacted by the editor of the business journal in my hometown. He inquired whether I could write a guest column for the next week's edition. I admitted that I didn't know how to do that, and he instructed me to write a column about anything that I thought would be of interest to people in business or those striving for success.

I hung up the phone and began dictating that first column to my colleague, Dorothy Thompson, to whom I have dictated more than 20 books, numerous movie scripts, and literally hundreds of these columns over the years. That first day, I merely shared some thoughts off the top of my head, and 10 minutes later faxed them to the editor of the business journal. A few moments later, the phone rang and he inquired as to where I got that column or when I had written it. I assured him that I had dictated the column after his initial call, and his final instruction was to just do that every week.

In the ensuing years, that weekly *Winners' Wisdom* column that began as a feature in a local business journal has grown to the point where hundreds of newspapers, magazines, and online publications around the world carry the weekly column which is read by millions of people from every corner of the globe.

When Don Green, who runs The Napoleon Hill Foundation, contacted me about presenting some of my columns in this book format, I was excited about the opportunity. All of us who write books, make speeches, produce movies, or even submit a weekly column with the thought of making people's lives better, stand atop the giant shoulders of Napoleon Hill. Anyone who has written a self-help or personal-development book in the last 75 years enjoyed an advantage that Napoleon Hill never had. We have all benefited from Hill's masterpiece, *Think and Grow Rich*, and Napoleon Hill was forced to blaze that trail, breaking new ground within the science of human success.

One of my favorite authors, Louis L'Amour, often said, "No man can be judged except against the backdrop of the time and place in which he lived." When you consider Napoleon Hill in this light, his accomplishments are unparalleled.

This book has been compiled and presented in four categories by the fertile mind of Don Green and the expertise of my publisher Dave Wildasin. I am honored that these two gifted gentlemen have leant their talent, time, and energy to this project. Please note that the columns appear here just as they were printed in publications around the world. Some of them are more than a decade old at this writing, but the wisdom is eternal, and the context creates points of interest.

This book is designed with you in mind. Wisdom comes from experience, and most of those experiences are painful and costly. If you can learn from someone else's pain and expense, you are a wise person, indeed. I would encourage you to read this book, cover-to-cover, but also keep it as a reference text using the sections and individual columns as a resource you can revisit as your life journey calls for specific wisdom.

It is my hope that this is not a one-time encounter that you and I are having. My hope is, in the coming months and years as you travel toward your own personal and professional success, I can be your companion through these pages. Any time you need more encouragement or further confirmation of your own potential and eventual success, please reach out to me via email at Jim@JimStovall.com.

Thank you for investing your time and money in this book. I'm looking forward to a great return on your investment in your life.

JIM STOVALL
2014

I

WISDOM FOR THE SPIRIT

"Struggles often serve to release the wisdom, patience, and strength we all possess but too seldom demonstrate." —JIM STOVALL

WE ARE MUCH MORE THAN THE SUM TOTAL OF OUR PARTS. YOUR NET worth is more than money, and your value is far beyond what you realize. I have never believed that we are human beings seeking a spiritual experience. Instead, I believe that we are spiritual beings having a human experience.

The most talented, gifted, and well-connected people don't always win or succeed. Often, the least likely among us rises to the top. These intangibles are what complete the mind, body, and spirit package that constitutes who we are. All success begins in your spirit, and there is no success without a spiritual component.

THE BANNER OF SUCCESS

EACH OF US IS BORN WITH UNLIMITED POTENTIAL AND UNLIMITED options. As infants, we are quite certain that the entire universe revolves around us. Things are only important as they impact or relate to our lives. It's almost as if we were born with a banner that proclaims *I'm lovable*; *I'm capable*; and *I'm able to do anything I set my mind to.*

As time goes on, we make the mistake of allowing other people to write things on our banner. And they will write things such as *You're ugly; You're stupid*; or *You will never amount to anything.*

By the time we are through with our education and ready to commence with our lives, we are so burdened down with graffiti on our banner that the original message is often totally obscured.

No one can write on your banner or put a message into your mind that you will not accept. But in our own inadequacy, we often accept criticism from everyone and praise from no one. When people around us who know us well tell us we are special or valuable, we too often minimize this by simply stating *I'm lucky* or *I'm really not that great.* On the other hand, when a total stranger is rude or inconsiderate to us, we have a tendency to embrace their venom as something we deserve and embody.

Please remember that you were born lovable, capable, and able to do anything you set your mind to. Any other messages that you carry around with you are messages that you allowed someone else to write on your banner. Some of us need to begin to use the biggest mental eraser we can find in order to reveal the simplicity of the original message.

Today's the day!

A LESSON FROM A 4-YEAR-OLD

IF WE WERE TO CONDUCT A POLL AMONG THE READERS OF THIS COL-umn to determine how many of you could sing or dance, I fear that we would receive the overwhelming message that the vast majority of adults feel they have no talent in these areas. On the other hand, if we were to conduct the same poll among 4-year-olds, we would find that virtually all of them are convinced they can sing, and virtually all of them have confidence in their ability to dance.

Most of the 4-year-olds have little or no real talent, but, instead, they are endowed with incredible confidence in their own potential. This confidence, or certainty of success, is something we were all born with but we later traded in for a strong dose of what we call realism.

Shortly after we reach school age, we are taught lessons about the world that revolve around us, limiting our vision and becoming realis-tic. I defy you to find a statue or a monument ever erected to anyone because they were realistic. All dreamers, all achievers, all great people kept their child-like faith in their own dream and their ability to carry it out, and these great people had an inordinate gift to disregard the world's cries for reality.

I challenge you to go through a single day exploring every aspect, not from what is realistic, but instead from what is possible. If we can master this, we will begin to revert backwards and live our lives in the unlimited realm of the successful 4-year-old.

Today's the day!

The Right to Choose

TODAY WE ARE INUNDATED WITH TALK ABOUT ALL OF OUR RIGHTS. We hear about civil rights, equal rights, women's rights, minority rights, and many other worthwhile principles. But when you come right down to it, you and I only have one right in this world, and that is the right to choose.

We can't always choose what happens to us, but we can always choose what we are going to do about it. You are where you are in every area of your life because of the choices you have made in the past. Put another way, all of the choices you've made in your life, put together, have brought you to this place, at this time, reading this article.

As I travel around the world and tell many thousands of people each year that they are where they are in their lives, personally and professionally, because functionally that's where they chose to be, a lot of people don't like it. We have become a society of people that loves to blame someone else for our condition.

So when I show up and tell them they are where they are because that's what they chose, they tell me things like: I know my life's messed up, but if you knew my spouse, you would know why I'm in the shape I'm in. Or they will tell me things like: My boss is an idiot; The weather's too hot; The taxes are too high; I'm a middle child, or whatever the current excuse is that they use to justify their life of mediocrity. Only when we accept the fact that we are where we are because of choices we've made in the past can we live every day of the rest of our lives in the certain knowledge that we can do anything we want to do if we simply make the right choices. Your destiny awaits.

Today's the day!

KEEPING UP WITH THE JONESES

AS YOU MAY KNOW, WHEN I AM NOT PURSUING MY PASSION OF SPEAKing, writing books, making movies, and developing these columns each week, I am in the television business. It is important for you to understand how the media and big business views you. You, by virtue of the fact that you are breathing, are lovingly known as "a consumer."

Consumers, in the minds of media and big business, exist for the sole and singular purpose of buying goods and services. Whether you buy the appropriate goods and services is not nearly as important—in their minds—as how much and how often you buy. For example, in the television business, programming or the show you watch is nothing more than a vehicle designed to keep you tuned in to the next commercial. Your newspaper is filled with ads, and your mailbox is stuffed with notices from companies clamoring for you to buy their trinkets.

> *If you are not happy now, there is no specific thing*
> *that you are going to purchase that will make you*
> *happy. Don't confuse "having" with "being".*

Please understand that there is—in and of itself—nothing wrong with working hard to acquire goods and services that you want. This is the American way. It is, indeed, what makes our economy and world go 'round. But don't be confused with the things you really want out of this life and the things that big business and the media tell you that you want. We are bombarded with messages that tell us if we can only drive the right car or wear the right brand of jeans or drink the right beverage, we will have, indeed, arrived.

If you are not happy now, there is no specific thing that you are going to purchase that will make you happy. Don't confuse "having" with "being". The media would tell you that having goods and services is the ultimate in this life. The reality is, having comes from doing; and doing comes from being. Resolve to be the kind of person you want to be who will then do the kinds of things that you wish to do in this life that can result in your having the things that you really want.

Focus on the being, not the having and you will find happiness as well as all of the consumer goods and services your heart might desire. Make sure the things you pursue are those things you really want, not your attempt to keep up with the mythical Joneses.

Today's the day!

THE THINGS WE DO

FROM TIME TO TIME, IT IS PRODUCTIVE TO EXAMINE WHY WE DO THE things we do. Not so much the big things, but the day-to-day tasks that account for many of our professional and personal hours. Too often, we get caught up in "doing things the way we've always done things" or "doing things the way we were told" or doing them "the way the manual said to do them." In the vernacular, this is known as "thinking in the box."

While there is certainly nothing wrong with doing routine tasks in a routine way, periodically, we need to examine why we do them—particularly in light of our goals and objectives.

We've all heard the story of the mother baking a holiday ham for Easter. Before she put it in the pan, she cut the end off the ham and set it aside. Her young daughter who was working with her in the kitchen asked a logical question. "Why do you cut the end off the ham before you put it in the pan?" The mother replied, "That's the way we've always done it." The young daughter, not being subject to the mental paralysis that most of us live with, inquired as to why it had always been done that way. Forced to think about it, the mother realized she didn't know. It was simply the way she had been taught by her mother.

During the elaborate dinner, the mother turned to her mother and asked why she had cut the end off the ham before putting it in the pan. The response was much as you would expect. "That's the way we always did it."

When the question "Why?" persisted, she decided to go to the phone and call her mother who was living in a retirement home. When the matriarch of the family was asked why she had always cut the end of the ham off and had taught her daughter to do the same, which had been passed down to her granddaughter and great-granddaughter, she laughed heartily and responded, "When I was a young bride, I only had one small pan, and I had to cut the end off the ham in order to accommodate the pan."

Although this story has been told many times, it is prudent for us to think about how we invest ourselves in the day-to-day tasks that confront us.

Today's the day!

EXPECT THE BEST

I HOPE THAT I AM NOT THE FIRST PERSON TO INFORM YOU OF THE solemn and inevitable fact that life is not fair. Unfortunately, we do not always get what we want or deserve or earn. We do, however, inevitably get what we expect. We move inexorably toward our most dominant thought.

It has been said a hundred ways by great men and women over the last five thousand years of recorded history that we are what we think about. Many times, success or failures become a habit. People who seem to move from tragedy to tragedy in their lives, becoming ever-more beaten down, will often be heard to say, "I knew that was going to happen." On the other hand, the winners in every arena of life seem to continue to win time after time and expect it as their due.

As we go about our daily lives, it is important to remember that we always find what we're looking for. If you set out today thinking that this is going to be a bad day, shortly things will begin to order themselves to meet your expectation. Conversely, if you set out with an expectation of greatness, this can be one of the greatest days of your life.

Ironically, the circumstances may not change, but we always find the result we are seeking. How many great days do we all miss because we are too busy highlighting the negative things around us to revel in the wonderful things life gives us?

Please do me a favor. For one day, expect great things to happen; look for them at every turn; and watch them come to pass. By the time you put your head on your pillow, you will have enjoyed an exceptional day. If my system does not work for you, you'll be happy to know it comes with a money-back guarantee, and you will have all the days of the rest of your life to expect, look for, and live through the worst.

Life isn't so much what happens to us as it is how we perceive what happens to us. I wish you a life full of whatever you expect.

Today's the day!

NOTHING AND EVERYTHING

MY MOST LASTING MEMORY OF THE OKLAHOMA TORNADOES IS OF A young father being interviewed on the radio. As he stood with his wife and two children on the spot of barren dirt that hours before had been his home and everything he owned, he spoke the words I will keep with me always. He said, "We have lost absolutely everything. We have nothing left other than the clothes on our backs." Then, after a brief pause, he continued, "But I guess we are lucky since our whole family is safe and sound. We have everything important."

To have lost everything and still have everything seems contradictory, but it's not. As I reflect on the lessons presented by the young father, I realize that we all spend a lot of time accumulating things that in the final analysis have little importance. And often, we don't understand what is really precious until the less significant things are gone.

The devastated areas would be rebuilt and restored; the broken, shattered lives would be put back together; and the families who have lost loved ones would somehow find the strength to go on. As a people, we seem to define ourselves during the most trying times. Within hours of the tornadoes, nameless volunteers appeared and worked tirelessly and selflessly for days. Truckloads of food and supplies were gathered and rushed to those in need. Emergency crews, government and private agencies, as well as churches and nonprofit organizations all had their finest hour.

Sometimes we seem to be at our best when life deals us its worst.

The capacity of people to dig out from the rubble of their shattered lives and dreams and—within a few days—be building back, bigger and better, makes us all proud. But let us never forget that, when you've lost everything that you own, but you still have your friends and family around you and the desire to go on, you still have everything.

Today's the day!

The Key to Happiness

In this day-to-day existence that we commonly call life, there are those rare and special moments when we rise above the fray and experience our true destiny. When it is all said and done, I believe that—more than anything else—life is about being happy in the active pursuit of making others happy. Most people are too busy making a living to really have a life. Happiness is often elusive and fleeting.

There are three elements that, when combined, always result in happiness. Like a three-legged stool, they work in tandem. Any two of the three are sorely lacking when the third element is absent.

In order to be truly happy in the largest sense of that word, we must have something to do, someone to love, and something to look forward to. Given those three things, we will find ourselves experiencing happiness and joy. Take away one or more of these elements, and we are but groping in the dark for that elusive, missing, intangible, undefinable "something" that we only know exists because we don't seem to have it.

"Something to do" represents the investment of the most precious commodity that we all have—our time. We all have the same amount of hours and minutes each day. Success and happiness hang in the balance based upon how we invest our time. Many people think that paradise would be a wonderful tropical island where there was nothing to do all day. Great literature is full of examples of people on such islands, totally invested in the pursuit of escaping.

"Someone to love" represents the investment of esteem and caring that we invest in others. In order to experience happiness, we must emotionally get outside of ourselves to affect the outcome of other people's lives.

"Something to look forward to" is the investment of hope and energy we put forward into a time that has not yet arrived. No one can truly be happy who lives only in the here-and-now. We have to accept the fact that there is more to this existence than we currently have in front of us.

The next time you find yourself experiencing that life of "quiet desperation," examine your soul and determine whether you're missing something to do, someone to love, or something to look forward to. Therein lies the key to your happiness.

Today's the day!

You Are Not Your Performance

We live in a totally results-driven society. You are only deemed to be as good as your most recent victory. This has set up a consistent state of low self-esteem for many people.

Recently, I enjoyed the NCAA National Championship Basketball Tournament. For months, every team in the country has a goal of making it to the tournament. Then, at the end of the season, 64 teams are selected from various parts of the country. As the tournament progresses, teams are eliminated one-by-one until, at the end of the season, the team remaining is named the national champion.

Among all of the participants who began at the beginning of the season, and among all the top 64 who actually made the tournament, only one team comes out on top. If this is our only goal, the majority of us are doomed to failure. *Success lies in the balance between seeking and striving on one hand and being peaceful and content on the other.* This balance can only be achieved when we separate our self-worth from our performance.

Small children seem to innately understand this. It's okay to have fun while playing a game whether you win or lose when you're six years old. Unfortunately, as we grow up, it's not okay to lose because we become identified with our performance.

> *Success lies in the balance between seeking and striving on one hand and being peaceful and content on the other.*

We all have value that has been placed inside of us. That value is totally separate from our performance. You can read any day in your local newspaper about great athletes, successful movie stars, or champions within the business world whose personal lives are total failures. Their performance may be at a peak level while their lives are not.

Never make having things or achieving status as your goal. Instead seek to be the kind of person who will naturally do the right thing that will result in all of the things that our culture calls success.

Today's the day!

DON'T MISS THE MESSAGE

TOO MANY OF US GET CAUGHT UP IN THE COUNTERPRODUCTIVE PRACtice of getting hung up in details while missing the big picture.

I remember as a small child hearing the story about Jonah and the whale. This story has a number of significant principles that can impact our lives today. Recently, I was listening to one of the all night radio talk shows. I heard a group of scholars and a number of callers from around the country debating issues regarding Jonah and the whale. Questions ranged from "Was it really a whale or a big fish?" to how Jonah could stay alive for three days under water even while inside a whale, a fish, or whatever it may have been.

As the conversation and debate droned on, I realized that these people were hung up in the details and were missing the big picture. They were debating fine points that can never be fully confirmed or denied while missing the pertinent message that can apply to everyone. A messenger doesn't have to be perfect in order for us to receive a powerful message.

Gandhi said, "Every man is my superior in that I can learn something from him."

Immediately after the Watergate incident, Richard Nixon became a much-maligned public figure. Everything he said and did was scrutinized and discounted because of the well-documented details of the Watergate case. Later in life, Nixon redeemed himself, to a certain extent, and became a well-respected author, lecturer, and elder statesman. People came to recognize that while Nixon had made mistakes, as we all do, he probably possessed the greatest mind relating to international affairs of anyone of his generation. For many years after the Watergate incident, everyone totally disregarded what Nixon had to say because he became a flawed messenger.

Gandhi said, *"Every man is my superior in that I can learn something from him."* This is true and, furthermore, every experience, situation, book, conversation, etc., can teach us something.

All the details do not have to be fully defined or fully understood for us to receive value. The messenger may be unknown or totally flawed, but the message may have validity. Therefore, we must, in every situation, ask ourselves, regardless of the details, circumstances, or the messenger, "What can I learn from this, and how does this apply to me?"

Today, vow to seek wisdom and knowledge from every source, not just the ones that you fully understand or the ones that meet some arbitrary standard of society.

Today's the day!

A MAN CALLED "TREMENDOUS"

I HAVE A DEAR FRIEND WHO PUBLISHED MY FOURTH BOOK. HIS NAME is Charlie "Tremendous" Jones. Charlie came by this unique name when he wrote a book many years ago entitled *Life is Tremendous*. If you are a regular reader of *Winners' Wisdom*, you know that I rarely recommend a specific book, but if you want to experience everything life has to offer, Charlie's book is a must-read.

We spend a great deal of time, effort, and energy worrying about what other people think of us. Really, the opinions or labels we give ourselves are the only ones that truly matter. Think what it must mean to go through life with everyone around you calling you "Tremendous." This would affect you every day whether you realized it or not.

How often do we hear other people call themselves lazy, stupid, ugly, etc., after they have made a common human mistake? We all do things we feel good about as well as things we are not proud of every day. The messages we tell ourselves are what's important. We are not our performance, nor are we the thoughts and feelings of others around us. We are, instead, the embodiment of the labels we give ourselves.

Imagine if instead of thinking "I'm stupid" when you make an error, you simply said or even thought to yourself, "I am tremendous, but that was not a tremendous thing I did." This simple change, compounded hundreds and thousands of times over months and years, will change the way you look at yourself. Then the way you identify yourself will change your expectations. Your expectations will change your actions. Your actions will change your habits. Your habits will change your character. And your character will redefine you.

If you don't have a name to subconsciously give yourself, I would like to loan you Charlie's. I do not have his permission to loan his name to you, but anyone who is "Tremendous" certainly wouldn't mind. Today, as you go through your routine tasks, remember to think of yourself as "Tremendous." Identify yourself as "Tremendous," and you will instantly notice changes in yourself and the world around you.

Charlie Jones was right. "Life is Tremendous."

Today's the day!

The Opinion that Counts

We always live up to the expectations that we have for our lives. Sometimes, these expectations are those we have of ourselves, but too often these are expectations that we allow other people to place upon us. If we're not careful, we can find ourselves winning someone else's battle while we lose our own war.

For years, societal pressure and the media have encouraged us to keep up with the Joneses. Unless your last name is Jones, there is no practical or logical reason you should set your standards based on theirs.

After many of my speaking engagements, I have the opportunity to meet with people one-on-one about their career and life goals. Too often, these seem to be pre-packaged, cookie-cutter goals that we have all been sold. Sometimes, it's necessary to get away from all of the external input and pressure to simply reflect on "what is really important to me in my life."

Assume that money, time, education, and other factors do not enter into your life goals. We all know that eventually these factors do count, but it is important that we not get the "How are we going to do it?" mixed up in the "What are we going to do?" decision.

We spend so much of our time, effort, and energy trying to insure that others will think the best of us. I don't think we would worry near as much about what other people thought of us if we realized how seldom they actually do think of us.

The way to build a great life is simply to string together a series of great days. A great day can be defined as one in which, as you put your head on the pillow, you can reflect back over your day's activities and be satisfied. Ideally, you are not only satisfied with how well you did in pursuing your goal, but you are deeply satisfied that you are pursuing the right goal.

Make a commitment to pursue the things that really matter for you and your family. Let the rest of the world try to keep up with the Joneses, whoever they may be.

Today's the day!

Priorities and Schedules

EACH OF US ON A DAILY OR WEEKLY BASIS SOMEHOW REDUCE OUR activities to a schedule. Some people use formal organizers or planners; others scribble notes on blank sheets of paper; and still others use obscure systems that defy description. But, in our own way, we each come up with a mental or literal "to do" list for the day.

As we examine our list of activities each day, we generally prioritize them. That is, we determine which of these activities is the most important and which can wait till later if necessary.

Recently, I was on a business/pleasure trip and had some time to contemplate priorities. Not only the priorities in my business life, but my life priorities as well. I found that the things that are most important to me in an overall sense rarely, if ever, are included in my daily list of priorities. I realized that I have been making the mistake of prioritizing my schedule instead of scheduling my priorities. There's a big difference here I hope you will grasp and apply to your life.

How many of us have been waiting to take that three-day weekend or have a special lunch with an old friend, etc., until time was available in our schedule. You know the old story as well as I do: Time is never available, and things only happen when they are scheduled. For this reason, in order to be a successful human being, we must take the life priorities that we all have and make sure they all fit into our schedule. Our business activities can expand to account for the entire day unless we first and foremost schedule our priorities.

Time for family and personal growth should be blocked out in our calendars before the daily crush of activities is allowed to take over our lives.

Remember that yesterday is history, tomorrow is a mystery, and today is a gift. That's why it's called "the present." Be sure to live it that way and plan to live it that way in the future.

Today's the day!

A BOX FULL OF STUFF

ALL OF US GO THROUGH THOSE SEEMINGLY INSIGNIFICANT POINTS IN life that, in retrospect, are turning points. I remember the day that our family came to the decision that my grandfather could no longer live in his house alone, but would need to move into a retirement center. He was well into his 90s and had called that house his home for over 60 years. It was full of trinkets, mementos, personal treasures, and memories.

On the fateful day he was going to move approximately 200 miles to another city where more of our family could be close to him, we made arrangements to make the move as easy as possible. You will be happy to learn that, as a blind person, I don't drive, but I am blessed to have a limousine and a driver. I sent the driver to pick up my grandfather and all of his "stuff" in the limousine. My grandfather had ridden in the limo several times, but—as a product of the Great Depression—he never could quite get comfortable with it; however, as it is the most spacious automobile imaginable, I thought he would need the room for all of his "stuff."

When the driver returned and let me know he had successfully deposited my grandfather at the retirement center, I asked if there had been enough room for all of his "stuff." The driver laughed and replied, "He only had one small box, and I just sat it on the seat beside me."

I called the retirement center to make sure he had everything he needed. The staff assured me everything was in place. Although over the next few weeks and months, my parents did bring my grandfather several other items they thought he might need, it struck me that after a whole life of acquiring "stuff," his basic needs boiled down to one box.

This prompts us to ask ourselves: How much of what we think that we really have to have are things we need? And how many of the things we are seeking are simply different kinds of "stuff" that the media or society has sold us?

Our basic needs are very simple. "Stuff" beyond that is either icing on the cake or baggage that weighs us down. Make sure that you have your "stuff" instead of your "stuff" having you.

Today's the day!

THE BEST IS YET TO COME

I HAVE A FRIEND WHO, FOR YEARS, HAS ENDED ALL OF HIS CONVERSA-tions and correspondence with the phrase, "The best is yet to come." This is more than a pleasant platitude. It leaves you with the positive expectation that it's going to be a good day.

As our population ages, our society is looking at the prospect of caring for older bodies and minds. The critical element of the quality of one's life is not how old is your mind and body, but how old or renewed is one's spirit. We all know people who are elderly in their spirit in their 20s or 30s. On the other hand, like me you have probably met people in their 80s or 90s who are still young at heart and full of life. I believe the difference lies in my friend's motto, "The best is yet to come."

We become old in our attitudes when we begin to believe that our best days or the best things in life are behind us. We begin to cling to memories instead of the expectation of tomorrow. On the other hand, no matter what age we may be, if we assume "The best is yet to come," it becomes a self-fulfilling prophesy and will insure us a great day ahead.

We have spoken before in these little visits I call *Winners' Wisdom* about the three elements necessary for happiness: Something to do, someone to love, and something to look forward to. If we can live with the expectation that "The best is yet to come," we will always have something to look forward to, and we will find it much easier to identify something to do and someone to love.

We all have tough times and bad days. The difference lies in how we look at these experiences. Some people view difficulties as the normal course of their existence. Others look at troubles as a brief parenthesis in life that will be followed by exciting things and better days.

Remember, we don't always get what we want, need, or earn. We do, eventually, get what we expect. Go through today with the highest of expectations, and you will, like my friend, discover that "The best is yet to come."

Today's the day!

My Guitar Gently Weeps

OVER THE PAST TWO WEEKS, I HAVE LOST THREE VERY SPECIAL PEOPLE in my life. Between all of the funerals, memorial services, and eulogies, I have been in a reflective mood.

This morning, I got up early for my ritual workout session. As is my habit, I turned on the radio to have some music to accompany my exercise. The first song was the classic "Something" by George Harrison. A giant no less than Frank Sinatra called this tune his very favorite. Next, they played another Harrison tune "Here Comes the Sun" which always leaves me positive and hopeful. Finally, they played the third Harrison song in a row. They played "While My Guitar Gently Weeps." The haunting instrumental duet between George Harrison and Eric Clapton was the original motivation for many of us who enjoy playing and/ or listening to wonderful guitar music. As the song slowly faded away, an emotional announcer stated that "George Harrison passed away last night at age 58."

Harrison was the youngest, and probably least well known, of the four Beatles. He got his first guitar when he was 13 years old, and several years later taught John Lennon how to play. Their guitar collaborations taught a lot of us how to play. Whether you like Harrison's music or not, you would at least have to admit he left a lasting legacy for the world.

There are very few people in each generation who come to embody the thoughts, feelings, and spirit of their contemporaries. George Harrison accomplished this. For better or for worse, at the turning of the next century, people will be listening to George Harrison melodies. The long view of history will judge him and his accomplishments. The reflection of time will help him to settle into his rightful place in the history books.

What is important for you and me is to realize that time is moving on, nothing is forever, and we must each seek out the legacy we will leave. In the final analysis, it is more important how you change the lives of those whom you touch every day than whether or not you change the world. In fact, we each change the world every day when we touch the lives around us.

Pursue your dreams as if you will live forever, and consider your legacy as if this will be your final day.

Today's the day!

CORNERSTONES

SEVERAL YEARS AGO WHILE I WAS SPEAKING TO A GROUP OF YOUNG people, I was presented with a dilemma. I was explaining to my audience of pre-teens that it is vital to always stretch ourselves and grow into tasks that we have never attempted. One particularly energetic young man asked if there was anything I wanted to do that I had not attempted. Before I could think about it, I heard myself say, "I've always wanted to write poetry."

He echoed my words back to me, saying, "It is vital to always stretch ourselves and grow into tasks that we have never attempted." For your consideration, here is the first of many poems I have written that will always be dedicated to that young man.

If I am to dream, let me dream magnificently.
Let me dream grand and lofty thoughts and ideals
That are worthy of me and my best efforts.

If I am to strive, let me strive mightily.
Let me spend myself and my very being
In a quest for that magnificent dream.

And, if I am to stumble, let me stumble but persevere.
Let me learn, grow, and expand myself to join the battle renewed
Another day and another day and another day.

If I am to win, as I must, let me do so with honor,
humility, and gratitude
For those people and things that have made winning possible
And so very sweet.

For each of us has been given life as an empty plot of ground
With four cornerstones.
These four cornerstones are the ability to dream,

The ability to strive,
The ability to stumble but persevere,
And the ability to win.

The common man sees his plot of ground as little more
Than a place to sit and ponder the things that will never be.
But the uncommon man sees his plot of ground as a castle,
A cathedral,
A place of learning and healing.

For the uncommon man understands that in
these four cornerstones
The Almighty has given us anything and everything.

Today's the day!

Beyond the Barrier

All of us have fears that we face. These fears cause us to do certain things and cause us not to do other things. Fear is a very natural and normal response in most cases. However, from time to time it is important to ask ourselves, "Are my current fears well-founded concerns that are keeping me out of trouble or are they irrational thoughts that are keeping me from where I should be?"

Many people in our society have a fear of flying. Their fears range from an uneasy feeling just before takeoff to stark terror that keeps them from even going near an airport. A certain degree of fear with respect to flying is good. If you are going to take a very large metal contraption that weighs many tons and fill it with people and then thrust it into the air, a proper degree of concern, caution, and prior planning is important. On the other hand, if someone is missing all of the many benefits that modern air travel can afford because of an irrational, unfounded fear, it may be worth looking into.

I will admit to having a certain degree of fear as it relates to skydiving. I feel I have resolved this in my life as I have absolutely no desire to jump out of an airplane with nothing between me and death but a piece of fabric. Since I have no real need or desire to skydive, the fear I have really does not affect me in any significant way. On the other hand, if I had a fear of meeting new people or going new places, it would be something I would have to deal with in order to pursue my passion and my destiny.

In the final analysis, the determining factor must be our own goals and pursuits. If the barriers we have allowed to build up in our minds are keeping us from pursuing the best that life has to offer, it's time to make an adjustment. Remember when you were young and you were afraid to dive off the diving board, ride a bicycle, or go to school by yourself? These were very real fears at that time in your life, but if you had given in to them, think of all that you would have missed. If the fear is keeping you from your destiny, remember that greatness lies just beyond the barrier.

Today's the day!

A Lesson from the Fish Tank

At my house, there are no dogs or cats as our travel schedule would make that sort of pet ownership difficult; however, for the past few years, we have been the proud owners and caretakers of what has become an extremely large tropical fish. Recently, we were advised that he would do better if he had a larger tank. So, we doubled his living space by purchasing a new aquarium.

After preparing all the assorted chemicals and paraphernalia necessary to open a new fish tank, on the appointed hour we ceremoniously dipped him out and put him in his new home. Even though there was twice as much space as he had previously enjoyed, he simply swam around in a small, confined space within the corner of his new aquarium. He had obviously become accustomed to living in a small space.

Many of us make this same mistake in our personal and professional lives. We assume that the future is limited by the past, and our capacity cannot be stretched or expanded. Too often, our rationale for pursuing a familiar course is simply the fact that it is familiar. The statement "We have always done it this way" is heard far too often.

It took the fish several days to slowly expand his horizons and occupy his entire new home. But after several weeks, I am pleased to report that everything is well within our fish aquarium. I am certain that in a short period of time this new tank will become the norm, and if we were to transfer the fish to an even larger aquarium, we would go through the same growing pain and adjustment as before.

A small bit of success in the past can limit our future. We spend too much time looking back at how we succeeded on a larger scale than we had ever known before, but we often fail to look forward to the future and explore how we can make tomorrow bigger and better than today.

Our past is useful to learn from and build upon, but history should never be used to define the future. Realize that each day starts as a blank page. Make it count.

Today's the day!

TOMORROW IS NOT THE DAY

THOSE OF YOU WHO ARE REGULAR READERS OF THIS ONGOING EFFORT of mine know that each of my columns ends with the phrase *"Today's the day!"* This is a constant reminder that yesterday is nothing more than a passing memory and tomorrow is nothing more than a hopeful promise. Today holds our only existence.

We, here in Western civilization, have failed to master the concept of living in the moment. We spend so much time worrying about yesterday or planning tomorrow that we fail to live today.

Think about trying to live your life "on purpose." This means really do what you're doing with your whole mind, body, and spirit. Don't be doing one thing and thinking about doing another. This conscious effort to "live in the moment," will make you better at the things you do but, more importantly, will cause you to examine the significance of the tasks on which you decide to invest your time.

> *Remember that this moment of this day is all we really have. As always, today's the day!*

One of the reasons we let our minds wander into the past or the future is because we are all guilty of filling our days with mundane and mindless activities. Some of these are unavoidable, but we must constantly eliminate as many of the time-wasters as possible. A life lived to its fullest is nothing more than a series of years, months, weeks, and days lived in the same fashion. Somehow, when we project into the future, we only think of things that hold a great deal of significance to us.

Our future can only be significant if we build it on top of the meaningful tasks that we perform today.

Remember that this moment of this day is all we really have. As always, *today's the day!*

CIRCLING THE WAGONS

ALL OF US OWE A GREAT DEBT TO THOSE BRAVE SOULS WHO FACED unknown frontiers as they crossed the North American continent in covered wagons. It's likely that wherever you live, the earliest settlers came to your area in this primitive fashion or in some quite similar method. There is much we can learn from these bold and visionary individuals.

One of the practices of the early wagon trains that we can apply personally and professionally in our lives is the circling of the wagons. Whenever they were attacked, the long wagon trains would alter their column formation and form a circle. Within this circle of wagons, the most precious people and possessions were gathered in the middle to be protected by less valuable items that could be sacrificed if it became necessary.

Although all of the possessions within the covered wagons were valuable, these settlers found that there was even a higher level of priority within their own value hierarchy. They were willing to sacrifice needed tools and implements and even their wagon to save first their family members and then valued family heirlooms and treasures.

It might be meaningful for you to undergo a brief exercise. Imagine your house is on fire. List the ten things you would most want to save from the destruction. These may or may not be the things you would think that you would most highly value. It is enlightening, from time to time, to imagine a personal or professional crisis and think of those people and things that are valuable and dependable that you would wish to surround you.

I am often reminded of the early mountain man who roamed freely throughout the Rockies far before that area was settled. He was able to move unencumbered along beautiful mountain trails where very few people had ever been able to go. Years later in his life, he had obtained more possessions and wealth. While traveling through the area in a wagon, he was forced to take a desert road instead of his beloved mountain trail. As he gazed at the beautiful mountain peaks in the distance, he realized that his quest for a few material things had changed the course of his travels and the course of his life.

If we are not careful, often we can find ourselves striving to obtain or maintain associations and possessions that are less valuable than the ones we are sacrificing in our futile quest for things we don't want.

Today's the day!

WRITING YOUR OWN OBITUARY

THOSE OF YOU WHO ARE CONSISTENT READERS OF THIS REGULAR offering realize that I rarely recommend specific books. Instead, I encourage people to read those books that will help them in the pursuit of their own passion. However, recently I have completed both of Tom Brokaw's books dealing with the Depression and World War II era—*The Greatest Generation* and *The Greatest Generation Speaks*.

Those of you who lived through those times, or were raised by someone who did, will find both books a wonderful and refreshing trip through the best and worst of times. For those of you of more recent vintage, you will discover a generation of people who shaped the world we live in today through their character, integrity, and determination.

As you experience the various stories of people affected by the Depression and the second world war, you will be struck by the fact that they did not realize they were living through history. They felt they were just simple people doing their jobs.

As we go through our day-to-day activities, we, too, often fail to realize the significance of the time and place in which we live. Each of us, every day, is living out our own biography. We rarely think of it this way until we read a friend's or loved one's obituary. Then the span of a lifetime is put into a manageable perspective.

How would you live your life differently today if you knew that it would become a permanent part of history or at least be read as your obituary by your loved ones at the end of your life? Think of things in the day-to-day ebb and flow as permanent sign posts along the course of history. You never know which may be the significant intersection until you are far beyond the point where you can do anything to change it. Assume that every activity in which you choose to invest your effort is of powerful and significant importance. When you take care of the little details, the big things automatically fall into place.

If you do not feel that kind of passion or importance for the things you do on a daily basis, either find something new to do or a new attitude about the course you are on. There will come a day when people read your obituary and consider the mark you have made in this world. On that day, it will be too late to make a difference. Make your mark while you can.

Today's the day!

THE GIFT OF PROBLEMS

ONE OF MY MOST POPULAR BOOKS IS ENTITLED *THE ULTIMATE GIFT*. It is a novel that deals with discovering the 12 gifts that make our lives complete and fulfilled. Readers instantly understand the Gift of Family, the Gift of Friends, the Gift of Money, etc. The one gift that baffles most people at first glance is the Gift of Problems.

It is important that we realize that in every tragedy and in every problem, there is a potential gift and a seed of greater good. This is what I call the adversity advantage.

While tragedies such as the terrorist attacks of 9/11 have caused great pain and suffering, there are potential benefits that can come from the devastation. Who among us did not feel closer to friends and family? Who among us did not feel more patriotic and a heightened sense of pride in our country? Who among us has not come to value the job done by police, fire, and emergency workers?

The damage is done. There is nothing any of us can do to reverse the death and destruction. What we can do is commit ourselves to moving forward with a new sense of appreciation for the life we live and the freedoms we have.

Those who tried through senseless acts to destroy our spirit and our freedom have, instead, rekindled an even deeper appreciation for these things among all freedom-seeking and peace-loving people around the world.

When we think about the adversity advantage, it is important to remember that the adversity carries no automatic benefit with it, but our reaction to the adversity can make all the difference. For every person you can show me defeated by circumstances, I will show you another individual facing the same circumstances who has turned the adversity into an advantage and moves forward as a better, stronger person with a heightened sense of destiny for their life.

Today, begin to look for the adversity advantage in the current circumstances.

Today's the day!

The Gift of a Day

YOU MAY RECALL THE OLD SONG LYRIC, "WHAT A DIFFERENCE A DAY makes."

A day can transform everything that comes after it. If you will think of your past and the days that have been pivotal to bring you to where you are now, you might think of your wedding day, your graduation day, the day you started a new career, etc. Some of these pivotal days simply happen, and others we plan and work on for many years. In our society, we have come to call a "normal day" one in which nothing pivotal happens. However, it's important to note that if you are on the right course, pursuing the right destiny, these "normal days" are important.

Like me, you can probably recall an exciting basketball game coming down to the wire. In the last few minutes, the two teams battle back and forth and, in the final second, a shot goes in the basket to win the game. That shot will come to be known as "the winning shot." In reality, any basket scored from the opening tip-off till the final buzzer would have won the game. We simply choose to focus on the final basket.

There are days when we cross the finish line, reach the goal, or pass the milestone. These are special days, and we should enjoy them. But don't ever forget the ancient Chinese proverb, "A journey of a thousand miles begins with a single step." Every step along the way is to be experienced, enjoyed, and savored.

The Gift of a Day is just one of the special gifts in my book and movie, *The Ultimate Gift*. I hope you will take that journey with me.

Today's the day!

THE GIFT OF DREAMS

DREAMS ARE THE STUFF THAT MAKE UP OUR LIVES. WE ARE EITHER IN the fortunate group of people who are living out our dreams, or we are those restless, wondering individuals who are living the proverbial lives of quiet desperation.

I am not talking about daydreams or fantasies. We all have those fleeting glimpses of ourselves playing center field for the New York Yankees or the Arizona Diamondbacks, as the case may be, in the final game of the World Series. I am, instead, talking about dreams as a future visualization of how our lives could be or should be.

As young people, we all had those things we wanted to be or do or have. They were the dreams of our youth—the visualizations of our destiny. By the time we are an adult, functioning member of society, most of us have diminished our dreams or forgotten about them entirely.

Young people formulate their dreams as the choices among all the possibilities in the world. As we get older, we narrow our dreaming capacity to those things that we currently have the ability or the wherewithal to achieve. It is important to realize that the biggest dreams we ever had in our lives are still alive and well, and within the realm of possibility.

I always take the week between Christmas and the new year to reconnect with my dreams and goals. Often, throughout the year, it is hard to get away from the day-to-day rush and really think about the things that are important. We are so busy making a living we forget to create a life. The life we're living right now is not a practice game. This is the Super Bowl and the World Series and the Olympics all rolled up into one. If you do not feel that kind of power and passion each day of your life, this would be a good time to dust off those old dreams and find your unique and fulfilling place in this world.

The Gift of Dreams is just one of the twelve life gifts in my book and movie *The Ultimate Gift*. I hope you will begin to explore each of the gifts and embrace your life as The Ultimate Gift.

Today's the day!

GETTING EVEN OR GETTING AHEAD

RECENTLY, I HAVE BEEN STUDYING THE ART OR SCIENCE OF HEALING. Healing is generally thought of in the physical sense of being sick and getting well. While this is certainly a valid part of healing, it barely scratches the surface. If we only look at healing as a method to get something back that we have lost, we have missed a great lesson and tremendous potential.

When you study stories of people who have gone through great struggles in their physical body, their personal life, their business life, or any other arena, they will invariably tell you that the road back to wholeness may or may not exist, but the road to a greater good has definitely been a part of their healing.

Who among us would not want to have the physical body you had as a teenager? But would you want to go back and face everything else that went with those years and the struggles you have gone through between then and now? You may never get back to where you were, but you will always have the opportunity to get ahead.

The stock market has resembled a roller coaster, sometimes on the down side of a great mountain. People have experienced tremendous financial losses. Those who will fare well are those who look at financial loss as an opportunity to learn and get ahead. Those who focus merely on getting back what they lost will, most often, be disappointed; and even if, over time, they are successful, they will merely arrive back where they started.

Every obstacle in life comes with a corresponding lesson and the seed of a greater good. Embrace the struggle and view healing as more than simply restoration—but, instead, as a life lesson in the great resources you already have inside of you.

Struggles often serve to release the wisdom, patience, and strength we all possess but too seldom demonstrate. Rarely are people at their best when circumstances are good, but when tragedy strikes or obstacles appear, you will find superhuman traits being displayed. In the aftermath of terrorist attacks, the goodness and even the greatness of people across the country became so commonplace as to no longer be newsworthy. Today, as you face disease, stress, struggles, or obstacles, embrace the experience and ask yourself, "What is the lesson and where is the advantage?"

Today's the day!

WORRY VS. CONCERN

I BELIEVE THAT CONCERN IS WORRY WITH ACTION. WORRY IN AND OF itself does nothing other than diminish focus. Concern has the potential to release creative solutions to the obstacle that one is facing.

I heard a story about an elderly monk who was training a number of younger monks learning to live their dedicated lives of service. One of his pupils came to him and told him that he was so weighted down with all of his worries that he could not perform his tasks. The old, wise monk said, "I have a gift for you. It was given to me by an old and wise monk when I was your age. This gift has allowed me a life of grace, peace, and focus."

At that point, the older monk handed the young man a worn and battered wooden box with a slot cut into the lid. The young man barely disguised his doubt when he asked, "What possible good could a box like this do to help me alleviate all of the worries in my life?"

The wise old man explained, "This box is a tool. Like any other tool, in the hands of someone who knows how to use it, it is most useful and effective." The old man went on to explain that the purpose of the box was to hold all of one's worries. Throughout the week, when confronted with any trouble, problem, or worry, the old monk would simply write down the issue at hand on a slip of paper and put it into the box. Then, once a week, he would dedicate a morning to going through all of the slips of paper accumulated throughout the week. After 40 years of pursuing this practice, the old monk had discovered that the majority of problems and worries solve themselves long before the week is out.

Problems and worries fall into three categories. One are those that we can do nothing about. Two are those which resolve themselves regardless of our worry. And the third and final group of problems or worries are those that we can affect with our actions. These are the problems where we should focus our energy. Our energy will turn these unproductive worries into productive areas of concern.

Focus and action are the keys. Take the worries out of your daily life, and schedule them in once a week. Take your concerns and act upon them immediately.

Today's the day!

THE RACE OF YOUR LIFE

WE ALL REMEMBER THE TRAGIC DEATH OF RACE CAR DRIVER DALE Earnhardt. Whether you are a fan of that sport or not, you were probably impacted by the terrible accident that took his life.

Since the tragedy happened, there have been endless debates about the safety of the sport, whether or not it's too dangerous, and exactly how Dale Earnhardt died. I do not wish to debate the merits of auto racing, safety issues, or even exactly how Dale Earnhardt died. Instead, I wish to explore how Dale Earnhardt lived his life and impacted those close to him and the entire world.

Dale Earnhardt died just as he lived—pursuing his passion and competing in a sport where he was among the very best. It has been argued that, if there were no automobile races, Dale Earnhardt would still be alive. The argument could be made that, if he could not pursue his destiny, the Dale Earnhardt the world came to love may never have been alive.

Everyone I have heard remembering or eulogizing Dale Earnhardt since the accident has expressed one, consistent sentiment. That is that Dale Earnhardt died the way he would have wanted to. This is not to say that he had any type of death wish or did not treasure his life the way the rest of us do. This simply means that he left this world while pursuing his dreams and competing the only way he knew, which was "all out."

I know that there will be efforts to make auto racing safer, and I hope that each of us will remember to buckle our seatbelts and take all reasonable precautions as we go through life. But, in the final analysis, none of us is going to get out of this world alive. It is much more important how we live than how we die.

Each day is a gift, and we never know when our time may be up. I hope all of us end our last day on this earth pursuing the thing we love the most with all of the energy and passion we possess. If we can do this, it will be our own small memorial and tribute to Dale Earnhardt.

Today's the day!

FINDING YOUR PLACE

IF YOU DON'T KNOW WHAT YOU'RE DOING IN THE WORLD, HOW WILL you ever know what in the world you are doing? We all meet people every day who are like the arrow in search of the elusive target. As the Cheshire cat in *Alice in Wonderland* taught us all, if you don't know where you're going, it really doesn't matter which path you take. I believe that each of us has a life's work or a destiny that is unique.

It is fun to observe people who are pursuing their passion. They have a joy and an energy that is infectious. On the other hand, we all have encountered people who are obviously not passionate about their daily tasks. Their attitudes can also be infectious, but it is certainly not positive.

Your passion and destiny may lie in a totally different direction from that which you are pursuing. On the other hand, you may be very close to the right path, and a bit of a fine-tuning will get you there. When you find that destiny, it's like putting your foot into your shoe—it simply fits.

In the over-priced, over-publicized, over-indulged world of sports, it is refreshing—if rare—to observe someone who simply loves to play the game. Several years ago, I read Lee Trevino's biography titled *Super Mex*. In this book, Lee Trevino describes the grueling pace of the professional golf tour. He explains that after being out on the road playing tournament after tournament for several months, there's nothing he enjoys more than getting home and simply resting—at least for a day. But as Lee Trevino recounts, "By the next morning, you will find me somewhere near my home on a golf course. I just love to play this game."

I would encourage you to pursue your passion. If you don't know what that is, you need to pursue discovering your passion. In one of his most famous songs, John Denver wrote, "Going home to a place you've never been before." This is the experience you will have when you find your destiny. Everything in your life will seem to fit, and the whole world will slide into focus.

More people fail because they are pursuing the wrong goal than those who simply fail to achieve the things they really desire. Find your destiny.

Today's the day!

SUSPENDING DISBELIEF

YOU MIGHT BE SURPRISED TO LEARN THAT, AS A BLIND PERSON, I AM A huge fan of Broadway theatre. Whether I am in New York or catch one of the touring companies on the road, I love the experience. I have been to dozens of shows and have gone backstage many times to explore the sets and props. It never ceases to amaze me that a vaguely painted piece of canvas with a few spotlights can turn into the Paris Opera House or colonial Philadelphia or even pioneer day Oklahoma.

In conjunction with my work at the Narrative Television Network, I have had the privilege of interviewing a number of Broadway stars as well as creative people behind the scenes. The success of Broadway theatre, they tell me, depends upon the audience's willingness to "suspend disbelief." This means that the audience believes the setting and the circumstances because they want to. As one sits in the darkened theatre, the desire to get caught up in the story makes the experience possible.

> *We can live out our wildest dreams and greatest imagined successes if we will simply suspend the disbelief that is keeping us anchored to our current mediocrity.*

I wonder how this same suspension of disbelief might apply to our personal and professional lives. Suppose, instead of just going through the motions of our daily, mundane tasks, we saw these activities as stepping stones toward making our dreams come true. Further suppose that when we thought about our dreams and goals, we stopped listening to those voices around us saying, "That's not real" or "That could never work in your life." If instead, like in the theatre, we were willing to suspend our disbelief and dismiss skepticism, I believe that we would find a whole new world of possibility.

If the simplest of settings and costumes can take us anywhere in this world or even to a new world within the confines of a theatre, why can't the same principles work in our daily lives? The magic doesn't end at the footlights. We can live out our wildest dreams and greatest imagined successes if we will simply suspend the disbelief that is keeping us anchored to our current mediocrity.

Assume this is possible. Give it a try, and you will not only enjoy the theatre but enjoy every day of the rest of your life.

Today's the day!

RELEASING CREATIVITY

SOME OF THE MOST HAPPY, WEALTHY, AND SUCCESSFUL PEOPLE IN our society are those individuals who are creative. I believe everyone has the ability to be creative in some arena in life. Some individuals find outlets within which to release their creativity. Other people never do. Creativity may range from writing the great American novel to putting together an intricate business deal to creating a culinary masterpiece for you and your guests at a dinner party to hitting a great golf shot to save par on a difficult hole, and virtually every other range of human activity.

If you ever feel as if you're not creative, it may be because you are trying to release your creativity in the wrong area. Most experts would agree that Michael Jordan was among the greatest basketball players ever to play the game. His highlight film would certainly qualify him for what I would call a creative genius. But when Michael Jordan decided to be a baseball player, he could only manage to be a mediocre Minor League player. While it's remarkable that someone could switch sports and still be competitive at all, his creative genius was only evident in one area.

What if Picasso had never painted, or what if Beethoven had never composed? Would they have been known as creative geniuses in other areas of life? I believe that they have given gifts to the world for generations to come because they found their unique creative outlet. How, then, can you and I find our creative outlets? I believe it is a matter of removing everything that is not your creative outlet, and that which remains will be your passion in which you will excel.

I always enjoy remembering the story about the Renaissance sculptor who bet a friend that there was a beautiful girl playing a harp inside a solid block of marble. His friend took the bet, and the sculptor began chipping away. It wasn't long before the beautiful girl playing the harp emerged. His friend, while paying off the bet, asked the artist, "How did you know she was in there?" The artist replied, "I could see her with my creative eye. All I needed to do was to get the rubble out of the way." You and I have the ability to create masterpieces in our own field. But we must get the distractions and assorted rubble out of our way.

As you go through your day today, look for ways to think and act creatively. Within your personal and professional life, an artist will emerge.

Today's the day!

ABOUT THANKSGIVING

ONCE A YEAR, WE ARE ALL FOCUSED ON THANKSGIVING. FOR A LOT OF us, this focus comes down to the three Fs. Family, food, and football. While I enjoy all three of these things and believe Thanksgiving to be a wonderful part of the year, it is easy to miss the significance of the season. By the significance of the season, I do not mean only commemorating the pilgrims landing on Plymouth Rock and surviving the harsh winter. As significant as this is, I also mean taking time to reflect on the gifts we have in our lives and the many things for which we should be thankful.

Thanksgiving, for many people, has become part of a blur that begins before Halloween and rushes through into the New Year. Holiday flows into holiday with little time to catch our breath and rest our credit cards. It might be prudent for you and me to leave Thanksgiving alone as a celebration of the three Fs and select a more unencumbered time of year to really think about our lives and be thankful. Better yet, instead of setting aside a holiday each year, wouldn't it be better to set aside a brief period each day?

In one of my books, *The Ultimate Gift*, I wrote a chapter about The Gift of Gratitude. In this chapter, I describe a daily ritual that has been adopted by scores of people around the world. It has become known as "The Golden List." The pursuit of "The Golden List" is simply the process of taking a few brief moments preferably in the morning to mentally list 10 things for which you are thankful today. I discovered this process purely by accident, but it has become one of the more meaningful parts of my day and one of the more significant messages it has been my privilege to share with my readers.

Before you begin your hectic workday filled with personal and professional tasks, designed to create more wealth, success, and happiness in your life, it is good to take measure of the amazing things you already have in your life. This brief accounting in the morning makes it virtually impossible for you to have a bad day.

As you go through your day today, realize that billions of people have lived on this planet for thousands of years. Most of them would have given all they had to trade places with you today.

Today's the day!

LESSONS FROM LITTLE ONES

CONVENTIONAL WISDOM WOULD TELL US THAT, AS CHILDREN AND young adults, we go through a period of education, maturation, and learning. We grow in wisdom and experience with each birthday. Hopefully, the process of collecting knowledge and applying it in our lives becomes an ongoing lifelong pursuit. Contrary to this notion, however, is the fact that there are some things we mastered as small children that we somehow lost along the way.

I regularly speak before arenas, convention centers, and corporate meetings in front of thousands of people. These people are mostly upwardly mobile, intelligent business leaders. They have all been well educated and well trained.

Let's say, during one such presentation in front of 10,000 people, I asked for volunteers from the audience to come up on stage and sing a song, do a dance, or draw a picture. How many of these 10,000 well educated people would you think would rush up on stage to demonstrate their talents? I'm sure you can agree with me that it would be far less than one percent. On the other hand, what if—instead of these mature business leaders—we had a group of five year olds? When we called for volunteers to sing, dance, or draw, how many of these kindergarteners would volunteer? You and I both know it would be virtually all of them.

Most of the adults would give the excuse that they have no talent in any of these creative arts. On the other hand, the kids don't know and furthermore don't care. The children are willing to express themselves without fear of consequence. This is an asset we all had that most of us have long since lost. Somewhere along the line we got the message that unless you can do something competently or professionally, you shouldn't do it at all.

Intellectually we understand that in order to do anything competently and professionally, you must first be willing to do it poorly. This lack of willingness to be vulnerable relegates most adults in our society to move farther and farther down an ever-narrowing road. They are not willing to try new things and experience that which is outside of their realm of comfort.

As you go through your day today, look for new things and experiences you would like to add to your life. Be willing to be vulnerable enough to be bad in the beginning so you can perform masterfully in the future.

Today's the day!

EXPANDING THE HORIZON

I HAVE JUST FINISHED A FASCINATING BOOK ABOUT THE LIFE AND VOYages of Ferdinand Magellan. Between 1519 and 1521, he led the first voyage that sailed completely around the globe. Although he was killed before the voyage ended, it was his vision and leadership that made this unparalleled feat possible.

You are probably asking yourself, "What does this have to do with me, here in the 21st century?" Always a good question to ask. I believe that history has a lot to teach us about humanity, both good and bad. Good things from history can save us time as we move toward our goals in life. Bad things from history can help us to avoid the pitfalls. Lessons not learned from the past are certain to be learned in the future as history repeats itself.

Magellan, in a small 50-foot boat, launched out into uncharted waters on a voyage the scope of which has never been duplicated before or since. At a time when there was still debate as to whether or not the world was round—and even if it were round, were there navigable routes to circle the world—Magellan began his epic trip.

The only current analogy to Magellan's trip would be to launch you into space at the speed of light to an unknown galaxy where you would have to find food and fuel in order to stay alive and make your way back to earth. While none of us are prepared to take on an adventure of that magnitude, we must constantly expand horizons in our own mind, body, and spirit.

We should all commit to an ongoing expedition within our own personal and professional development. What things are you going to know, master, create, or achieve in the coming months and years that are beyond your known horizon today? Before we are able to expand the things we plan to do in the future, we must first open our minds to expanding the possibilities that exist before us. Just because you haven't gone somewhere before in your life doesn't mean that place or achievement or goal does not exist.

> *We must constantly expand horizons in*
> *our own mind, body, and spirit.*

As you go through your day, seek to expand the horizons or the realm of possibility in your life.

Today's the day!

YEARS OF LIFE

RECENTLY, I GOT THE SHOCKING AND DISTURBING NEWS THAT A DEAR friend of mine is facing a life-threatening disease. A million things immediately go through your mind when you get this kind of news. First, you think of what this friend means to you and how their loss would impact your own life and the world around you. Then you go through the parade of thoughts about family, friends, business concerns, and an endless stream of images that assault you.

Thankfully, my friend received an early diagnosis, a quick and successful treatment, and a positive prognosis. Thankfully, above all, my friend is a fighter. If you were taking bets right now on who might live to be 100, I would put a serious wager on my friend's chances.

After the immediate shock and fear that comes with the potential life-threatening news, we all begin to assess our own lives. We are left with the reality that my friend is going to die, I'm going to die, and, my dear reader, you are going to die. As important as it seems to all of us—how many years of life we have—what is infinitely more vital is the question of how much life is in our years.

We all know people who are in their 80s or 90s who are full of life, joy, and optimism. They are looking forward to great things ahead, and they are excited about what life has to offer. On the other hand, we all know people who are barely out of their teen years or early adulthood who seem dull, listless, and have a negative outlook toward the days ahead. I think one of the factors that differentiate the positive from the negative people is how they view the best days of their lives.

Negative people at any age somehow believe the best times of their life are behind them. They are in the process of dying, no matter how many more years their heart continues to beat and how long they take up space here on our planet. Conversely, there are people who have lived a century of life here on earth. They have been everywhere, seen everything, and done everything but still they have a lust for life that energizes everyone fortunate enough to come in contact with them. These people believe that the best days of their lives are still ahead.

Death will find us all someday. May he find you and me excited, energized, passionate, and experiencing everything this existence has to offer. And as for my friend with the troubling diagnosis, he will continue to live life as the gift it is and make a difference for those around him. He will drink deeply from the nectar of life, and I look forward to sharing many of those drinks with him.

Today's the day!

THINGS THAT MATTER

IN THE AFTERMATH OF HURRICANE KATRINA, WE WERE SHOWN THE very best and the very worst of humanity. Crisis does not create character; it reveals it. We all have images or quotes that will be seared permanently into our consciousness of those who have experienced some of the worst that life has to offer.

I will never forget a gentleman who is a resident of New Orleans being interviewed several days after the storm. This gentleman described escaping New Orleans with his family at the last minute with no more than the clothes on their backs. Several days later, that family observed satellite photos of their house and everything they own submerged under 10 feet of water. The gentleman explained how they had lost their home, all of their possessions, their mementos, and their jobs. He went on to say, "We have lost just about everything." But then he chuckled and looked at his family and said, "But I guess we got out with about everything that matters."

This brings us to the question of things that matter. I believe that things in this life can be separated into two categories: Things that are valuable and things that matter. Things that are valuable would include your home, car, clothes, possessions, office, job, etc. These are all extremely important and significantly impact the way you live. Then there are the things that matter. They are your friends, family, hopes, goals, beliefs, and dreams. They impact us at a level that goes much deeper than status or possessions. They cannot be replaced.

I have come to the conclusion that no matter how valuable, anything that can be replaced with money does not matter—or at least should not be a treasure. It can be a valuable possession but when it is lost, we—like the man in New Orleans—begin to look toward the things that really do matter. Unfortunately, it often takes a disaster or life crisis to show us what really matters.

Many of us spend a lot of time working to acquire things that, while nice and valuable, don't really matter when compared to the treasures represented by our friends and family. It is sad to think that sometimes we can get caught up in the rat race of acquiring things to the extent that we diminish the things that really matter in our lives.

As you go through your day today, take a hint from our friends along the Gulf Coast. Enjoy the things that are valuable, but treasure the things that really matter.

Today's the day!

2

COMMUNITY FOCUS AND WINNING RELATIONSHIPS

"Treat everyone in the world as if they are a star, and the world will collectively make you a star."—JIM STOVALL

THE IMMORTAL WORDS, "NO MAN IS AN ISLAND," HAVE NEVER BEEN truer. It doesn't matter how gifted, talented, or well-educated you might be. You will succeed or fail as a part of a team, and you will find happiness and contentment as a part of a family, a community, and a society.

We find success when we help all the boats rise and elevate ourselves as we lift up those around us.

BECOMING A TOURIST AT HOME

OVER THE PAST SEVERAL MONTHS, I HAVE SERVED ON A CHAMBER OF Commerce Task Force dealing with conventions and tourism. The purpose of this task force is to explore how we can bring more tourists and convention dollars into our area. This has been an enlightening experience for me. I grew up here and thought there was very little I could learn about our community. I was wrong.

Through the process of studying how people around the country look at us, I have learned that we have many things to be proud of and many attractions to take advantage of here in our hometown.

Too often, I think that visitors or tourists get more out of a community than do the people who live there. This is because a tourist comes to a town with an open mind and wishes to maximize the time he or she will have in a city. I was surprised to learn that there are attractions that people come literally from around the world to enjoy that I was unaware of. I would venture to say that many people leave their hometown on vacation and spend a lot of time and money traveling a great distance to a destination with attractions that are no more desirable than the ones left at home. In fact, I can visualize people traveling down the highway with some magical destination before them, passing other people on vacation who are looking forward to a wonderful trip in the hometown that the first traveler just left.

Take the time to find out what is right here under your nose that you and your family have never experienced before you set off across the country. Call the tourism department and find out the wonderful things we have to offer here in our hometown. Don't get caught up in that old mindset that "You have to go out of town to really experience something great." There are people arriving here every day who thought the same thing about their hometown, so they have come here for a wonderful vacation.

I think you and your family could enjoy something totally unique on a regular basis right here in our area and virtually never run out of wonderful attractions. Make up your mind to be a tourist right here in your hometown. You'll find out that this is not only a great place to live, but also a great place to visit even if you do happen to live here.

Today's the day!

IT ALL STARTS WITH ONE PERSON

THERE'S A POWERFUL FORCE AT WORK IN OUR SOCIETY. I LIKE TO call it the "chain reaction," or to paraphrase Sir Isaac Newton, things that are set into motion tend to stay in motion. This can either be good or bad, depending upon the given action that starts the chain.

For example, have you ever pulled into a parking lot and found a whole row of cars parked on or over the lines? In your frustration, you might ask yourself, "How can this many people be rude enough to purposely take up more than one parking space?" The reality is that there weren't that many people being rude. They just fell into the "chain reaction."

Most probably, what happened is that one rude individual showed up early in the morning and—with total disregard for his or her fellow human beings—parked in such a way as to take up more than one space. Then the second person arrived and simply parked next to the first. Then the third, and so on. The next thing you know, the entire system is dysfunctional as the result of a "chain reaction" growing out of one rude person's actions.

There are really many people here who could have impacted the parking lot situation. Obviously, if the first person arriving had taken a little care and decided to be courteous, the "chain reaction" would have never started. But, it's important to realize that the second, third, or fourth individual arriving could have broken the chain by simply leaving a bit of extra room and parking within the next available marked space.

We all have choices every day. Hopefully, those of us enlightened enough to read *Winners' Wisdom* would never start a bad chain, but maybe even more important is the choice that we have to break bad chains. When someone deals with us discourteously, we have the choice to either act in kind or simply return their rudeness with politeness.

It is easy to act appropriately when we are treated appropriately, but the true champion of life will always take the high road, even when those around him or her do not. Make the commitment today to start good chains and break bad ones. The whole world will be a better place, and it starts with you.

Today's the day!

THE GIFT OF GRATITUDE

AN ATTITUDE OF GRATITUDE IS ESSENTIAL TO ANY LASTING SUCCESS. We must have the ability to look forward toward great triumphs, but, at the same time, look backward toward all of the people and events that have made success possible.

This week, I lost a dear friend of mine, Dr. Harold Paul. In addition to being an influential college professor, who gave me a passion for writing, Dr. Paul was a mentor of mine for 25 years. He had the unique ability to be both an encourager and a challenger at the same time. Every time in my life I reached a milestone, he would celebrate with me, but he would also challenge me to even greater heights. He gave me an expectation of even greater possibilities in the future.

I am grateful for so many things in my life, and the passing of Dr. Harold Paul has prompted me to stay in that attitude of gratitude for the things and people that have made so much possible for me.

Think of the things and people who have made the good things in your life possible. Take some time to reflect on them and, where appropriate, to express your gratitude. No one among us stands alone. The success you enjoy today and the vision that you have for tomorrow only exists because you have been privileged to stand on the shoulders of giants.

Take this opportunity to express your gratitude and to dedicate yourself to being an impactful person in other people's lives as a tribute to those who have given so much to you.

The Gift of Gratitude is just one of the twelve gifts making up my most popular book and movie *The Ultimate Gift*. I hope you will learn to give and receive gratitude as an integral part of success, and I hope you will invest some time and energy today into reflecting on and expressing your gratitude.

Today's the day!

LESSON FROM A LEGEND

ONE OF THE MANY PRIVILEGES ARISING FROM MY WORK AT THE Narrative Television Network is the opportunity to meet and interview really wonderful people from all walks of life. Many of these encounters were compiled into my second book entitled *Success Secrets of Super Achievers*. The thought being that success is a pattern; it can be observed, followed, and duplicated.

I am reminded of my interview with Steve Allen, who is probably best known for his work in television as the creator of *The Tonight Show* as we know it today. Few people know that Mr. Allen has written over 5,000 songs and has a Grammy Award to his credit. He has written 32 books, and he was working on his newest one the day I showed up to interview him at his office at the studio in California.

The most amazing thing I found about Steve Allen is that he is a very ordinary, common man. He felt most comfortable talking with the camera people and the crew, and was very unpretentious. When it was time for the interview, the attitude he displayed was "I'll do my job, and you do your job."

I believe he revealed the secret of his success when he said, "I try to never lose touch with the common man. I just visualize a guy at home watching television, and if I can come to him at his level, he will relate to me and feel good about me."

In his own way as a worldwide celebrity and one of the most talented and gifted people of our generation, Steve Allen has found the secret to greatness, which is his own personal form of the Golden Rule: Treat others as you would like to be treated. Not because it is some outdated theory, but instead, because you really believe everyone in the world has a vital function to perform, and everyone should be treated with respect.

As we go through our day seeking to elevate ourselves toward what we believe to be success, let us never forget the lesson from the legend, Steve Allen: Treat everyone in the world as if they are a star, and the world will collectively make you a star.

Today's the day!

PASSING THE TORCH

IN 1976, DURING A ROUTINE EYE TEST TO ENTER COLLEGE, I WAS DIAGnosed with a rare disease that would eventually result in my blindness. As a teenager with my whole life ahead of me, the devastation that I experienced was indescribable.

Several weeks later, a family friend called and offered to pick me up and take me with him to an event known as a "Positive Thinking Rally." I cared nothing about anything having to do with positive thinking, as I was settling into my own form of depression; but for some reason, I agreed to go.

That day, I heard Paul Harvey, Robert Schuller, Zig Ziglar, Art Linkletter, and Ira Hayes. When the lunch hour approached and my host asked if I wanted to leave for lunch or stay and hear a speaker named Dr. Denis Waitley, I was amazed to hear myself say, "I believe I'll just stay and listen to this guy."

In the midst of an incredible event with some of the greatest speakers of the 20th century, somehow Dr. Waitley reached forty rows back into that arena and lit a fire in me that has never gone out or even dimmed to this day. His words about the psychology of winning encouraged me to explore the possibilities of my condition instead of the limitations of my pending blindness. We have since formed a close friendship, and he continues to be my mentor to this day.

Dr. Waitley's inspiring message stayed with me, and although I did eventually lose my sight, I also became a national champion Olympic weightlifter, an Emmy Award winner, the president of a television network, one of the Ten Outstanding Young Americans, and the national Entrepreneur of the Year.

Look around you. Then reach out to someone,
and make a difference in their lives and yours.

The message is clear. In our personal and professional lives, we have the opportunity to reach out to hundreds of people every day—with an encouraging word, an act of kindness, or by simply taking a few moments to truly listen and help. We, as professionals, have a responsibility to positively impact the lives of others not only with our products and services, but by our examples. How much more effective we can be if, from time to time in the midst of our search for excellence, we stop to light a torch and pass it on to another messenger.

Look around you. Then reach out to someone, and make a difference in their lives and yours.

Today's the day!

SOME GET IT, SOME DON'T

HAVE YOU EVER NOTICED THAT IN THE MOST MUNDANE DAILY ACTIV-
ities, there are some people who get it and some people who don't?

When you are trying to merge onto the freeway during rush hour,
you will notice that most people simply move up into the acceleration
lane and politely and efficiently merge into the flow of traffic. They get
it. On the other hand, there are those few lost souls who want to stop at
the junction of the entrance ramp of the freeway and wait until traffic is
completely clear. They don't get it.

There are any number of these daily reminders of the fact that there
are certain universal, established, and accepted procedures that one must
master in order to fit into our society. Success and achievement are much
the same way. There are people who are totally motivated and have great
ideas, but there's one small, missing element they don't get.

Recently, I met a gentleman with a great concept for a new business.
He seemed to have everything necessary for success with the exception
of the fact that he wanted to do his own legal and accounting work.
This might be okay, except for the fact that he has no background or
experience in this area. Even if, by stumbling around, he could develop
contracts that did not get him into trouble or accounting systems of
his own that allowed him to track his money, he still is doomed to fail.
Every person whom he approaches with his new business will eventually
get around to asking to see some documentation or financial data that
will instantly reveal the fact that he doesn't know what he's doing.

His business has nothing to do with the practice of law or accounting, but he will fail because he refuses to follow what we all have agreed
upon as generally accepted methods. He simply doesn't get it. He doesn't
understand the rules.

It's like the tourist traveling in a foreign country who inadvertently through his language or behavior insults people by violating their local customs. He doesn't get it. The fact that he doesn't know he doesn't get it really won't matter to the people he insults.

Seek out people whom you trust, and ask them to be honest with you about every outward expression of your personal and professional life. Be sure that you get it and everyone around you knows you get it.

Today's the day!

YOU NEVER KNOW

I REMEMBER, AS A VERY YOUNG BUSINESSPERSON, THE FIRST TIME I dealt with a lawyer. We needed to get incorporated and, due to a referral, I found myself sitting before one of the most prominent attorneys in our area. I began by apologizing for the fact that I was nothing more than a start-up venture and would probably not mean much business for his law firm.

That attorney explained something to me that day that has stayed with me ever since. He said, "This firm is very large and successful because we have some very large and successful clients; but they didn't start out that way. Most of them came to us when they were in their initial stages of growth just like you. If there is any reason we are successful it is because we understand that little clients grow to be big clients. You can't always tell which ones will be big someday, so you have to treat everyone right all the time."

It's the same mentality demonstrated by a little boy standing outside of a television studio. When a good looking man in an expensive suit emerged, the boy held out his autograph book and pen and asked, "Mister, are you somebody famous?" When the gentleman assured him he was not, the boy thought for a minute and replied, "Well, why don't you go ahead and sign this anyway, because someday you might be famous."

In Joe Girard's book *How to Sell Anything to Anybody*, which in my mind is the bible of sales and marketing, Girard describes relational marketing. He explains that while attending a funeral he was handed a small card on the way into the service which told a lot about the life of the deceased. After the funeral, Joe Girard was speaking to the funeral director and happened to ask how people in the funeral industry know how many cards to print. He was shocked to learn that with rare exceptions, the average funeral has 200 people in attendance. Girard realized the significance of this, because if someone will take the time and effort to attend your funeral, you have influence over them. Therefore, we can assume that the average person you deal with on a day-to-day basis can influence the decisions of 200 different people.

The next time you even think of being less than polite and professional, instead of seeing one person in front of you, visualize all 200 people that they have influence over. You know who you know, but you may never know who they know.

Today's the day!

THE GIFT OF GIVING

TRAGIC WORLD EVENTS HAVE FOREVER CHANGED THE WAY WE LIVE, the way we feel, and the way we think. We have seen the very worst of humanity. Evil deeds have altered each of us, but not all of the changes have been bad ones.

There has been an emerging culture of giving that has brought renewed hope to anyone who is a consistent observer of the human condition. People have given money in unprecedented amounts. They have given their time, effort, and energy as volunteers and, when nothing else would do, they have given their own blood to assist victims that, in most cases, were unknown to them.

At its core, giving affects the receiver by virtue of the gift itself; but giving affects the giver in a much deeper and more lasting way. In the aftermath of an act of giving, the receiver has a new gift and the knowledge that someone cares deeply; but the giver has a new identity. He or she now has feelings of abundance, benevolence, and a sense of being able to make a difference—or at least communicate caring feelings.

Often, the greatest gifts are ones that cost very little or nothing at all. Just because something did not carry a sizeable price tag doesn't necessarily mean that it won't be treasured forever by the person who receives it.

You have heard it said that, "It's the thought that counts." This phrase is usually uttered after a gift has been given that may or may not be appropriate. In reality, whether it is the best gift ever or a useless trinket, it is, indeed, "The thought that counts."

A gift communicates that I thought about you, I care about you, and I wanted to share something with you. As you go through your day, find special and unique ways to give to those around you. It will show them how you feel, but more importantly, it will change the way you feel about yourself. The Gift of Giving is just one of the twelve gifts being offered in my book and movie *The Ultimate Gift*. I hope you will explore the Gift of Giving and each of the gifts that today has to offer.

When it's all said and done, the best gift any of us have is the gift of this day and how we share it.

Today's the day!

LESSONS FROM A FUNERAL

SOMETIMES, IN THE MIDST OF GRIEF AND DESPAIR, WE CAN LEARN lessons that help us to emerge as better people. Recently, I had the difficult task of speaking at a funeral for someone I really cared about. This experience caused a flood of emotions. Inevitably, on such occasions you reflect upon the brevity of life and the misguided priorities that we all pursue on a daily basis.

After the funeral, I had the opportunity to meet and greet a number of people. I was struck by the number of individuals who told me, "I really hadn't talked with her or seen her in over a year." And similar comments.

These are people who had not been in contact with the deceased recently but would take half a day out of their busy schedule to come to a funeral. While I am not critical of the fact that these individuals would pay their respects by coming to the funeral, I do believe that there is a lesson here for all of us.

> *Like any other positive thing in our life, staying in touch with those we care about should become a habit.*

Think of all the people that you may not have talked to or seen in months or even years. Ask yourself: If these people suddenly passed away, would I take several hours out of my schedule to attend their funeral? If your answer is Yes, why don't you take five minutes out of your schedule today to write them a quick note, send them a brief e-mail, or call them on the phone.

Like any other positive thing in our life, staying in touch with those we care about should become a habit. As human beings, we would like to tell ourselves that we do the right thing for the right reason, but rarely is this the case. I suspect that we brush our teeth more out of habit than a sense of dental health. I think we can express the love and care we have for those around us by taking a few minutes each day or week to contact a few of them. Then, the next time you're attending the funeral of someone you care about, you'll be able to say, "I had a nice talk with him just last week, and I'm so glad that I did."

Invest part of your day communicating with the special people in your life. It will pay great dividends for you and for them.

Today's the day!

KEEPING YOUR SANITY

HAVE YOU EVER HEARD SOMEONE SAY—OR EVEN CAUGHT YOURSELF saying—"That person is making me crazy"? This is a feeling we all experience from time to time, but it's important to realize that no one can affect us unless or until we give them permission to do so. The people who are closest to us have the greatest ability to affect us either positively or negatively. By virtue of the fact that they are someone we value either personally or professionally, we have automatically given them permission to have a great impact in our life.

For example, if you are walking along the sidewalk and a disheveled, homeless person in a severe state of intoxication stumbles up to you and says, "I don't like your shoes," this probably won't ruin your day, your next hour, or even occupy your thoughts beyond the immediate moment. On the other hand, if someone very close to you says, "I don't like your shoes," it may affect you greatly. You will either feel insulted and hurt or you will agree with them that there is, indeed, something wrong with your shoes.

All of us have imperfections, including those people whom we have allowed to be close to us and impact our lives. Let's say that someone you have a close relationship with is habitually late. This does not mean you cannot have a meaningful personal or professional relationship; it simply requires you to factor this into the equation. Assuming you have tried all positive and constructive ways to get this person to be on time, if they are still among the punctually-challenged, you have to be willing to deal with it internally.

If you are going to fret and yell and pull your hair every time this person is late, you are facing a lot of unpleasantness. The irony is that you will probably be the only one affected negatively. The person you are close to will breeze in 20 or 30 minutes late without a care in the world, and you will have allowed their tardiness to ruin your day.

We allow people to make us crazy when we don't allow them to be themselves. This is not to say that we shouldn't hold those we care about to a higher standard. It simply means if we expect perfection there won't be anyone in our lives, including ourselves.

Today's the day!

TOLERANCE

HAVE YOU EVER READ SOMETHING THAT FAILED TO IMPACT YOU AND then upon re-reading the same thing you find it to be revolutionary? This happened to me recently with a book by Napoleon Hill. This particular book contains a lot of excerpts from that legendary writer and speaker.

There was an essay entitled *Tolerance* that I know I have read more than once, but for whatever reason, I had not found it to be memorable. Upon my most recent reading, I discovered that it was one of the most significant things that Napoleon Hill ever wrote. The beginning of the essay is as follows:

> "When the dawn of intelligence shall spread over the eastern horizon of human progress, and ignorance and superstition shall have left their last footprint on the sands of time, it will be recorded in the last chapter of the book of man's crimes that his most grievous sin was that of intolerance."

Tolerance is nothing more than considering the other person's actions in light of their experience, background, and perspective. As human beings, we have a tendency to judge our own intentions but everyone else's actions. This sets up an impossible standard in our own minds that no one can live up to.

When we slight someone or perform in a sub-standard manner, we justify it in our own mind by saying, "I really didn't mean to do that. My intentions were good, but…." On the other hand, when someone slights us, we too-often judge nothing other than the action, and we are not willing to give them the benefit of the doubt as to their intentions.

As you go through your daily activities, try to be conscious of both your intentions and your actions as you deal with other people. Often we are unintentionally abrupt or rude to people when we do not mean to be. It is simply a matter of not being conscious of communicating our true feelings. When we are living our lives at our highest level, our intentions and our actions will be the same; however, we will often miss this mark, and we have to be willing to accept the fact that others we deal with will miss this mark as well. And we do not have the benefit of understanding their intentions. We only feel and react to their actions.

Before you react to someone's apparent insensitivity, ask yourself, "Do they mean to make me feel the way I am feeling right now?" You may even want to inform the person, "Do you realize that when you say or do that, it makes me feel like…?" Then ask, "Is that what you intend to communicate to me?" You will find that most misunderstandings are simply miscommunications. And then you will find it is much easier to practice tolerance.

Today's the day!

IF I WERE KING

SOMETIMES IT'S FUN TO IMAGINE HOW THE WORLD WOULD BE different if you were in control.

IF I WERE KING, people who did not vote would not be allowed to complain. The three good TV shows on each week would not be aired at the same time on different channels. Good weather would be given a priority on weekends and holidays. Telephone solicitors would only be allowed to call your house when you're not home; that way, they could talk to everyone's answering machine. Food that tastes good would be good for you. Junk mail would only come one day a month. Airlines would have to tell you the truth about when you were really going to leave—if ever. When a store advertised a half-price sale, it really would be.

I would average out our allotment of wisdom over the years of our lives. We would have more wisdom when we're younger, when we really need it. If I were king, we would have newer schools and older jails. Policemen, fire fighters, and teachers would be paid what they deserve. There would be enough handicapped parking spaces for everyone who needs one, but none left over. Everyone would be in the same time zone, and there would be a way to achieve Daylight Savings Time without the semi-annual disruption.

Road repairs would be spread out throughout the city and not concentrated in one small area. Everyone would be required to know all of their neighbors and talk to them on a regular basis. All the people on your Christmas card list would have to receive at least one call or visit from you during the year. Wars would be fought by the people who start them. Everyone would be required to work at something they enjoy.

And, finally, if I were king of the world, every man,
woman, or child would know that they were a
unique and special gift. Everyone would be allowed
to pursue their passion and maximize their talent.

IF I WERE KING, people would be required to spend as much energy on keeping jobs and relationships as they did on getting them. Elderly people would be highly sought-after for their wisdom and experience. Truth and good ideas would be popular, even if "We've never done it that way before."

And, finally, if I were king of the world, every man, woman, or child would know that they were a unique and special gift. Everyone would be allowed to pursue their passion and maximize their talent. But, since the odds are not great of my becoming King of the World, let's all do the best that we can.

Today's the day!

THE GIFT OF FRIENDS

SOME DAY WHEN YOU LOOK BACK ON WHAT I HOPE IS A SUCCESSFUL
and satisfying life, you will count your wealth not so much in dollars
but instead in the quality, caliber, and number of your friends.

> *It is simple to find people who will gather*
> *around you for a party or when times are*
> *good, but friendship should be measured by*
> *dependability in times of difficulty.*

The word "friend" is thrown about far too loosely in our society.
We have a tendency to think of those people with whom we have shared
good times as our friends. While many of these people are, indeed,
friends in every sense of the word, the best way to judge a friendship
is in times of difficulty. Think of those people you would call in the
middle of the night if you were facing a dilemma. There are those very
special friends that you know you could call at three in the morning
with a problem, and they would be there with whatever you need, no
questions asked. These are your friends.

It is simple to find people who will gather around you for a party or
when times are good, but friendship should be measured by dependabil-
ity in times of difficulty.

I remember as a small child being taught a valuable lesson about
being careful around strangers. I remember being told, "If you're ever
lost or need help, look for someone in uniform like a policeman or fire-
man." Those un-sung heroes that we too often take for granted have
been there and continue to be there when we need them.

Friends are not necessarily those with whom we can agree or those
who will be around us during the best of times. Friends are, instead,

those who we respect, and who respect us in times of disagreement while knowing all along that they will stand beside us in our darkest hour. Let us all make it a point today to recognize our true friends and treasure them as the gifts they are for a lifetime.

The Gift of Friends is but one of the 12 gifts in my book and movie *The Ultimate Gift*. I hope you will share each of them with me.

Today's the day!

THE SEARCH FOR NORMALITY

RECENTLY, I HEARD ABOUT A GROUP OF ADVERTISING AGENCIES THAT constantly seek what they call a "normal" city or town. Apparently, what they are looking for is the demographically perfect example of the United States. They spend a great deal of time searching for this elusive pocket of normality. Even when they find a city or town that they deem to be normal, within a year or two they have to move on, because the existing site is—for whatever reason—no longer "normal."

As young children, we are all born as separate and distinct creative individuals. No matter what you may hear to the contrary, our society does not reward or appreciate unique individuals. We are taught at an early age to conform in every way so we will not stand out from the crowd. In essence, we are taught to be "normal."

> *"Although you will never be normal, normal is really not anything worth aspiring to."*

This process of normalizing everyone is akin to seeking the lowest common human denominator. This is to say, if you never stand out you will certainly never be outstanding.

I will always remember being diagnosed with the disease that eventually resulted in my blindness. After it became apparent that I would slowly lose my sight and I would not be "normal," I remember my father saying, "Although you will never be normal, normal is really not anything worth aspiring to."

Although we would all agree with this in principle, as a society we still reward normality. While I would not advocate becoming anti-social; I do think that greatness comes from individual, creative expression. Think of all the things that you do throughout your day. Ask yourself what would happen if you began performing a few of these tasks at a higher-than-normal level. Look at the mentors or people whose performance you aspire to. You will find that the real achievers in this world rarely do anything "normally." They perform a few critical tasks at the highest possible level and, quite often, ignore or delegate mundane tasks to others.

Monuments are never erected to "normal" people. They are erected to people dedicated to doing one thing exceedingly well. Find that thing in your life, and avoid the temptation to be "normal."

Today's the day!

YOUR VOTE COUNTS

OUR VOTING SYSTEM IS UNIQUE IN THE HISTORY OF THE WORLD. While we are the only remaining superpower on the face of the earth, therefore making our president, in effect, the most powerful person alive, we must remember that any of us with our vote can control the fate of the most powerful person in our country and in our world.

I am hoping that all of us will see the significance of our right to vote—not only for president, but for all of the state and local matters as well.

I recently had the opportunity to read General Eisenhower's account of the invasion of Normandy on D-Day. Thousands of young Americans gave their lives on that day to defeat an evil dictator. What they were really fighting for, more than anything else, was your and my freedom.

A person who doesn't vote is no better off than a person who lives in a totalitarian system where he or she can't vote. If I could pass one piece of election reform legislation, I would make it a law that it would be a crime for anyone to complain about the government or any elected official if the person complaining did not vote. Get involved in the system.

Today's the day!

AN AMERICAN IN PARIS

I JUST RETURNED FROM SPENDING A WEEK IN FRANCE. I AM PLEASED to report that springtime in Paris is everything it is reputed to be. I would highly recommend the experience. I have always considered myself to be a proud American, but it took a trip abroad to give me a new and even deeper appreciation for America and Americans.

While in Paris, I took a day trip to Normandy. I visited Omaha Beach where our American troops landed on D-Day. A lot of attention has been brought to this historic event in the aftermath of the movie *Saving Private Ryan*. I had studied a lot about the Normandy Invasion and thought I had a good grasp of what transpired, but when I stood atop the cliffs on the French coast among the concrete barricades which had held the German artillery, I was awe struck.

I am convinced that the task of landing on that beach and getting to the top of the cliffs is among the greatest endeavors in the annals of human achievement. When you retrace the actual steps of the American young men who were there on that fateful day, you are struck with a sense of amazement that any of them actually survived.

Atop the cliffs where the Germans had their fortified bunkers, today is the home of a massive cemetery. I walked through many acres of white marble crosses, realizing that each represents someone's son, father, or husband. All of us value our freedom, but the value of anything can only be measured against the price paid to obtain it. Only when we remember that real people, much like you and me, paid the ultimate price can we truly begin to understand the gift we have been given.

On that day back in 1944, the world was at a crossroads. Some very special Americans performed an unbelievable task that liberated France, all of Europe, and broke the back of the Third Reich. That was the time and place that the Allied Forces determined to make a last stand for freedom.

The next time you sit in a darkened theatre or watch a video at home of *Saving Private Ryan*, please be reminded that there were thousands of Private Ryans and, over the ensuing decades and for generations to come, they gave you and me a priceless gift. May we all rededicate our efforts to take advantage of their gift and their sacrifice.

Today's the day!

THE GIFT OF LOVE

SINCE THE BEGINNING OF RECORDED HISTORY, HUMAN BEINGS HAVE struggled with the basic question, "Why are we here?" I'm not sure there is any perfect and final answer to this ongoing search for purpose and meaning.

The very best answer to the question, "Why are we here?" that I have heard comes from a treasured friend of mine, Debra Simon. Debra is the author and creator of a workbook and tape course entitled "Perseverance, Character, and Hope." In her tape course, Debra explains that we are here to "learn how to love." At first glance, this might seem to be an over-simplistic explanation, but when you really focus on it, you will understand that learning how to love encompasses every area of our daily lives.

Love is probably one of the most misused and overused words in our vocabulary. Many languages have multiple words to describe the various emotions that we lump into one four-letter word—love. During the course of a day, you will hear people say: I love my children; I love hotdogs; and I love my new big screen TV. While all of these are legitimate emotions, they are certainly not the same; therefore, it is understandable why there is some confusion when we try to act out of love in our daily lives.

Think of people in your past who have most often demonstrated the ability to act out of love. It may be a grandparent, a special teacher, or a dear friend. It is easy for us to have warm, loving thoughts toward these people. The real challenge in learning to love is to react this same way in situations where we don't feel loving and with people who are far less lovable.

When people attack us out of ignorance, fear, or hostility, our initial reaction might be to respond in kind. Even if justified, our non-loving response will continue the destructive cycle; however, if we can learn how to love and always respond that way in every situation, we can create a new environment around ourselves, and we will find that other people will begin to respond to it in a spirit of love.

The Gift of Love is just one of the twelve gifts in my book and movie The *Ultimate Gift*. I hope you will begin sharing the Gift of Love along with all of the gifts as you make today a special day.

Today's the day!

Perspective

Recently, I have been studying holidays around the world and how various people celebrate. The British tradition known as Boxing Day caught my attention. Boxing Day is celebrated the day after Christmas and, traditionally, involves the nobility offering presents to servants. Recently, I heard of the British military observing the holiday by having the officers and enlisted personnel exchange places for the day. In addition to being an interesting way to celebrate a holiday, there were many lessons to be learned by trading places with one's subordinates or superiors.

All of us realize intellectually that we are not an island and that whatever tasks we may accomplish are really a team effort; however, from time to time it is good to be reminded of this in real terms.

Those of you who are regular readers of my books or these columns would be interested to know that, while the ideas and concepts you read originate in the deep recesses of my mind, they arrive at the pages of books, newspapers, magazines, etc. through the talents of a very gifted person named Dorothy. Without the editors of newspapers, business journals, and magazines, you would never have read *Winners' Wisdom*. Those of you who have seen me speak in arena events or conventions have seen me standing there onstage all by myself. Without the ongoing efforts of a young lady named Kelly, these events would not be possible. If you have seen me on television, I was probably either by myself or interviewing someone. Without the significant contributions of creative forces like Beth and Susan in our studios, these television appearances would not take place.

In our offices, there is a very gifted person named Clover who makes everything happen, including the baffling task of making intelligent and useful information spew forth from our computers. And last, but never least, my partner, Kathy, is a world-class researcher and strategic thinker. Without her enlightened input, people around the country would find out what kind of executive I truly am instead of the extraordinary one that they believe me to be. I am blessed to have a wonderful team surrounding me who makes my dreams come true.

Think of your own situation. What are the things that you take pride in on a daily basis? Think of all the people who make that accomplishment possible. Be aware of their significant contributions and take today as an opportunity to simply say, "Thank you!"

Today's the day!

WHO ARE WE?

UNLESS YOU LIVE UNDER A ROCK SOMEWHERE OR HAVE BEEN ON AN extended vacation to a distant planet, you've probably heard more than you wanted to hear about the cloning controversy. You will be happy to know that I am not going to add my opinion to the myriad of people in the media who have offered you theirs. I do feel that the current controversy in media attention that has been surrounding the cloning and stem cell research, gives us the chance to explore some fundamental questions.

The most basic among these questions is the age-old quandary, "Who are we?"

For years, behavioral scientists have tried to quantify whether we are a product of our environment or our heredity. There has been more than enough said and written on this topic without bringing any conclusive direction to the debate. You will be pleased to know that, like the cloning issue, I am not prepared to offer my input as to whether we are a product of our environment or our heredity. I suspect the final answer would be somewhere in the middle, and we are probably a product of both our environment and our heredity.

> *If you knew that you were going to take on the characteristics of the people with whom you spend the most time, would you consider adding some more positive influences to your daily dose of friends and associates?*

For our purposes here, it is safe to say there is nothing we can do to change our heredity, and there is nothing we can do to alter the environment we have been exposed to in the past. Therefore, the only place where we can have an impact with respect to who we are, is our environment from this point forward.

If we knew, beyond a shadow of a doubt, that we would be changed and impacted forever by the people, places, media, and general environment around us, we might look upon these factors differently. If you knew that you were going to take on the characteristics of the people with whom you spend the most time, would you consider adding some more positive influences to your daily dose of friends and associates? If you knew that the books you read and the media that you are exposed to would alter your outlook, your direction, and your personality, wouldn't you begin to seek more positive input?

While science is wasting a lot of time and money debating questions that will never be resolved, I suggest that today, you and I focus on our world and the things we can, indeed, change.

Today's the day!

THE GIFT OF LAUGHTER

IT HAS BEEN SAID THAT LAUGHTER IS GOOD MEDICINE. OUR WORLD IS desperately in search of good medicine to heal wounds and conflicts.

When you think of the good times in your life and the special people you have known, those precious memories that you can recall most likely involve laughter. There are some memories that are so strong that just recalling a certain time and place can cause you to smile or laugh, even years later. These times are what I call "making a deposit in your memory bank."

If you doubt the power of laughter, I would refer you to Norman Cousin's book *The Anatomy of an Illness*. In this book, Cousins recounts his own story of overcoming a terminal disease through the power of laughter. It is not simply Pollyanna or pie in the sky; there are clinical, physiological benefits to laughter. But, more importantly, laughter improves the quality of the lives we live.

Kelly Morrison is the marketing director for my work on television, books, speaking engagements, and these columns. She is also a very talented singer and songwriter. The best song she has ever written, and one of the best that anyone has ever written, is entitled "Laugh a Little." The song is about two friends whose lives are taking them in separate directions. The parting advice is to always find a way to bring laughter and joy into every situation.

Find ways today to bring joy and laughter into your life and the lives of those around you. You will be healthier, happier, and a much more desirable person to be around. Particularly in times of stress, be sure to keep on hand: books, videos, and your ever-growing memory bank to give you an instant deposit of laughter and joy.

The Gift of Laughter is just one of the twelve gifts in my book and movie *The Ultimate Gift*. I hope you will embrace each of the gifts and focus this week on bringing laughter into your world.

Today's the day!

BRIDGES AND BOUNDARIES

IN EVERY HUMAN RELATIONSHIP, THERE WILL BE EITHER A SERIES OF bridges or a series of boundaries. Bridges are the trust emotions that link us to others. Boundaries are the distrust emotions that create barriers of perceived protection around us. Both bridges and boundaries will be tested by those we relate to as soon as they are established.

We have all experienced people who establish bridges at a rate we are not comfortable with. For example, if you meet a new neighbor who feels comfortable coming over to your house at all times of the day and night unannounced to borrow your things without permission, we could say that they have established a bridge that is not yet strong enough to support that element of your relationship. On the other hand, we all have friends of long standing who know that if they are truly in need, can come to our house at any hour and have anything that belongs to us that might help them. In this case, the bridge is strong enough to support that element of the relationship.

Boundaries work the same way. As soon as a boundary is established in a human relationship, it will be tested. If you tell your four-year-old not to get out of your yard, you can bet within a few moments, he or she will be at or beyond the boundary of your property. All bridges and boundaries will be tested.

Whenever possible in our personal and professional lives, it is better to build a bridge than a boundary. It is better to be involved with people you can trust because of the bridge you have built instead of only trusting them because of the boundary you have created.

The difference between being able to tell someone, "I trust you to handle this in the right way at the right time" is far superior than being forced to say, "Unless you perform in this fashion, I will be forced to penalize you." Given the opportunity, most people will strive to be trustworthy if presented with a bridge instead of a boundary. Obviously, we have prisons because some people cannot understand bridges and must be subjected to the ultimate boundary; however, most people will be as trustworthy as you expect them to be, and when you communicate the level of trust in your expectations, they will perform.

For over a decade as a blind person, I have given cash to literally hundreds of store clerks, hotel personnel, cab drivers, etc., many of whom already know that I am blind. To date, I have yet to have one person cheat me. If you go through life expecting people to be good, they generally will.

> *It is better to be involved with people you can trust*
> *because of the bridge you have built instead of only*
> *trusting them because of the boundary you have created.*

Today, find a way to build a bridge and tear down the boundaries. *Today's the day!*

It's a Small World

IF YOU WATCH THE EVENING NEWS AND SEE STORIES FROM AROUND the world, it is easy to get the impression that people are very different. While people from other parts of the world certainly live different lifestyles, they are very much a product of their environment. Their hopes, goals, dreams, and ambitions are very much like yours and mine.

Recently, I was contacted by a group that publishes business journals and periodicals in the former Soviet Union. They are making arrangements to translate these *Winners' Wisdom* columns into Russian, Ukrainian, Lithuanian, Estonian, and Latvian. My initial reaction was "Why would those people be interested in my weekly *Winners' Wisdom* columns on business, success, motivation, etc.?" But, after further reflection, I realized people are the same everywhere. They want better lives tomorrow than they have today, and they want a better future for their children and grandchildren.

These people around the world who are just beginning to experience capitalism and the free enterprise system are hungry for information and knowledge. While they are far behind us in methods and techniques, in the coming years, they will make up for this with their own burning desire and intense motivation.

We are truly in a global economy in a global society. Rapid, affordable transportation and the Internet are changing our world and the way we do business. In the past when you started a business, you had to decide how many city blocks or square miles would comprise your marketplace. Now, the World Wide Web gives us all the opportunity to be global instantly.

Often when we are considering our business, we think of ourselves or our next door neighbors. In the 21st Century, we must think of people halfway around the globe as well. In reality, with the new technology, these people are our neighbors.

As you are reading these words and considering how they apply to your success and your future, realize that people halfway around the world are reading these same words as they seek their own success. If you will focus on reaching your own goals by helping these people around the world reach their goals, you cannot fail. Life is still a matter of helping yourself by meeting the needs of others. Today, think about how your business can work on your block, in your city, and in every corner of the globe.

Today's the day!

PEOPLE AND EXPECTATIONS

AS YOU HAVE ALREADY DISCOVERED, THE WORLD IS FULL OF ALL KINDS of different people. Some of them mesh well with our personalities and expectations and others simply do not. This is not a problem in and of itself because all of these people put together make up our world as it exists.

The difficulty arises when we expect people to be other than what they are. For example, we all have a friend or acquaintance who is habitually late. If this is the only problem with a particular person, it can be dealt with. Over the months and years, we simply learn to build in extra time, because we know that they will continue to be late. The problem arises when we expect that late person to be punctual.

We can worry and fret over their being late, and they will still stroll in a half-hour past the agreed upon time. This becomes problematic, because invariably the person who is late is calm, relaxed, and doesn't have a care in the world while we—the person harboring the expectation that they will be on time—have made ourselves into a nervous wreck. It is a unique balancing act to expect the best of others while allowing them to be the people they have proven themselves to be.

Certain people will never be neat, thoughtful, polite, professional, or on time. This challenge is nothing compared to the one we face ourselves when we build a world of our own expectations that makes people what they are not. We cannot expect people to live up to our standards. We can simply point out what we consider to be a deficiency in their performance and make ourselves available to help them to the extent they really want help.

Most times, people who are late, rude, messy, unprofessional, etc. are that way because somewhere in life they have learned there is a pay-off for this kind of behavior, or the penalty is not sufficient enough for them to change. If instead of always complaining about your friend being late, you simply went on without them, they may begin to change their habits. Obviously, your complaints and your stress level have not worked up to this point.

Resolve to always expect people to do their best, but give them the latitude to be who they really are. In this world, there is only one person's performance that we can impact. Focus all of your energy on that person's performance, and allow other people to seek their own level.

Today's the day!

Six Occasions to Get It in Writing

As a blind person myself who has written a dozen books and hundreds of weekly syndicated columns over the years, I have to laugh when I think about how much writing I have produced. Even though I produce millions of characters of print that I can't read, I still understand that there are times you've got to get it in writing.

In your professional and even in your personal life, there are occasions when nothing will take the place of having black on white and ink on paper. Under the following circumstances, "always get it in writing."

1. If there is any question of integrity, don't fail to get it in writing. Please remember that there is always a question of integrity in a transaction. I am not doubting the honesty of anyone you or I might be in business with. It's simply that today, with countless mergers, acquisitions, and takeovers, the honest person that you made an agreement with may be out of the picture when the critical moment of integrity arises.

2. Getting it in writing will clear up failing memories. You may have closed a deal or entered into an agreement yesterday that is so significant and memorable you think you'll never forget what you committed to or what the other party promised. In reality, 18 months from now, you may not even recall that person's name. From time to time, I do business with friends and family. I always get it in writing. It's not because I don't trust these people. It's because I value the relationship so highly I don't want there to be hard feelings over one or the other of us having a lapse of memory.

3. When you're in an uncomfortable situation or a dispute that may result in conflict either personally or professionally, put your feelings and understanding in writing. Oftentimes, people get very sensitive in a dispute or misunderstanding. The wrong word or phrase can damage you forever. A word spoken in anger or frustration may never go away. Remember that if you put your understanding, feelings, or position in writing and present it to the other party, they generally have to read it in its entirety before they respond. If you try to bring up the same argument verbally, chances are you will be interrupted and be forced to deal with their argument, and no one gets to lay out their entire position. Communication is the key to most conflict resolution. Putting it in writing forces everyone to think and analyze before they speak.

4. If there is an agenda for a meeting or a follow up with specific tasks, always put it in writing. I have found throughout the years that the person who shows up at a meeting, negotiation, etc. with a written agenda for everyone controls the direction of the dialogue. Even if everyone doesn't agree with your agenda, at least everyone starts from your points and moves ahead from there. After a meeting or conference call, putting the various tasks and commitments of the various parties in writing will get you better results and performance. It will cut down on the amount of time you have to continue giving them the constant, annoying reminders of what they are supposed to do.

5. When you have an occasion to thank or compliment someone, put it in writing. It is a tangible reminder to them of your gratitude and esteem. If someone buys something from you or performs a task on your behalf, a handwritten thank you note will perform wonders. In the age of email and instant messaging, a handwritten note says more today than it did a generation ago. There are times to be high tech, but when you

are complimenting or thanking someone, it may be efficient but not nearly as effective.

6. If you have a goal for yourself, your team, or your organization, put it in writing and make sure that everyone involved gets a copy. People in our society have grown accustomed to making commitments in writing. If you buy a car, a house, or take out a loan, you cannot avoid signing reams of paper. We all take this seriously because if it is in writing, we know we are committed. There is nowhere that your total commitment is more important than your personal and professional goals.

Beyond these six points, whenever you're in doubt, put it in writing. If you don't need it, it didn't cost you much in time or money. If you do need it, it may prove to be priceless.

Today's the day!

3

FOCUS ON BUSINESS AND FINANCE

"Business, and life in general, is a balancing act between excelling in the current systems while creating new and improved ways of doing things and meeting the needs of those around us." —JIM STOVALL

BEYOND OUR NAME, WE ARE MOST IDENTIFIED IN SOCIETY BY WHAT we do for a living. After you are introduced to someone, identifying jobs and careers is the next bit of information you will generally exchange. You will likely spend more time working than you spend with your loved ones, so it is, therefore, imperative that you enjoy what you do, make a difference, and find fulfillment in your career.

The only people who make money work at a mint. The rest of us have to earn money. Money is only earned by creating value in the lives of others. If you want to generate more wealth, don't seek money. Seek more significant and deeper ways to serve more people.

Success is, inevitably, a win/win proposition.

THE GIFT OF MONEY

MONEY IS PROBABLY THE MOST MISUNDERSTOOD COMMODITY IN OUR society. People today understand the price of everything and the value of nothing. There have been more conflicts, divorces, and disputes over money than anything else.

In order to begin to have healthy attitudes toward money, we must understand that it is nothing more or less than a tool or a vehicle. Money can get us what we want or take us where we want to go. Unless there is something you want or somewhere you wish to go, money has no value.

Money is nothing more or less than a result of creating value in the lives of other people.

How would your life be different if money were no object? This is a difficult question to consider, because we seldom make any decisions that are not based upon money. This is a poor way to look at the world. Decide what is good or right or meaningful, and then worry about the money.

You may be interested to know there has never been a money shortage. There is, however, from time to time a creativity, service, or value shortage. Money is nothing more or less than a result of creating value in the lives of other people. If you will stop worrying about money and start worrying about creating value in the lives of those around you, you will have more money than you need. If you simply worry about money, you will never have enough. You will be like the foolish person standing in front of the stove saying, "Give me heat, and then I will give you wood."

The Gift of Money is just one of the twelve gifts featured in my book and movie *The Ultimate Gift*. *The Ultimate Gift* and The Gift of

Money teach us that everything we need to live out our biggest dreams and our ultimate destiny has already been provided for us. I hope you will begin to utilize The Gift of Money and make money your servant instead of being a slave to it. I hope you will pick up a copy of *The Ultimate Gift* and begin to see your life unfold as the fulfillment of your biggest dreams and your ultimate destiny.

Today's the day!

DOING BUSINESS WITH THE WORLD—ONE PERSON AT A TIME

IN THE BEGINNING, BUSINESS WAS DONE PERSON-TO-PERSON, IN THE form of bartering, or verbal contracts for personal services. I might trade you my camel for your baskets of wheat. Then we became "more sophisticated." Markets were set up, currencies were formed, and the medium of exchange became very complicated. People were relegated to doing business through established channels that were controlled by governments or big business.

The smallest business person was forced to do business through these channels in order to meet the wants and needs of his individual customer. For example, advertising in the media, doing business through the yellow pages, etc.

The Internet has changed and will eventually revolutionize the way we do business. It will not take us to a new level where we have never been before. It will, instead, take us back to the beginning. Many enterprising entrepreneurs are doing business from their home with nothing more than a phone line and a personal computer. They can do business anywhere in the world, day or night, with very few restrictions or limitations.

Many of us have tried to avoid or delay doing business on the World Wide Web. This is becoming less and less practical every day. People are simply not going to go through multiple layers of commerce when they can do business as it was done in the beginning—one on one with the customer.

These developments prove the validity of two old adages: "There is nothing more constant than change," and "There's nothing new under the sun."

If you want to revolutionize your business, your career, or your life, don't worry about the technology. Simply ask yourself, "What product, service, or information can I provide to people around the world?"

Even though the World Wide Web allows us to do business in the blink of an eye with thousands of people around the world, the dynamic is as old as the first trade. You must provide value in the exchange within a comfortable and pleasant environment to do business. In order to prosper in the 21st century, we must do business using the latest technology—and the most ancient methods.

Today's the day!

POWER OF PERCEPTION

AS A BLIND PERSON WHO HAS JUST FINISHED WRITING MY TENTH book, I have been contemplating the old adage, "You can't judge a book by its cover." I have come to the inescapable conclusion that people can and do judge books based on their covers and judge other aspects of life based on insignificant surface details.

In business, we all strive to promote and market our product or service. Hopefully, we are as sold on our company as we expect our prospects to be. But, in the final analysis, people don't do business with us based on our products or services, or even our ability to deliver those products or services. Instead, buying decisions that signal success or failure are based on prospects' perceptions of our ability to deliver products and services.

People who reject a book based on its cover will never know the treasures that may be inside. People who are true professionals and represent great products and services will fail if the perception of their ability to deliver those products and services in the marketplace does not equal the reality.

We have all had the experience of eating in a restaurant, staying in a hotel, buying a new car, etc. that did not remotely live up to our expectations because someone oversold and under-delivered. In order for the power of perception to work in your favor, you must, in fact, have the best product or service available anywhere. At the very core of your being, you must believe that if the prospect understood what you already know, you would have a permanent and mutually-beneficial relationship.

As you look at your business, first be sure that you are offering and delivering the very best available anywhere. And then, try to look at the perception of your business objectively. What do people experience when they meet you, come into your place of business, talk with your co-workers and colleagues, read your correspondence, etc.? This is what will, inevitably, determine your fate in business and in life.

Be sure that you are proud of your product and your ability to deliver it. And then, make sure that the perception in the marketplace matches the pride, care, and professionalism you put into serving your customers.

Today's the day!

COST AND VALUE

PEOPLE IN OUR SOCIETY TODAY KNOW THE COST OF EVERYTHING AND the value of virtually nothing. We treasure things that bring us very little, if any, pleasure, and we ignore the truly priceless.

When you establish your financial goals, it is important that they really be "your goals," not someone else's. We are constantly bombarded with messages that tell us to feel good or be important we must drive a certain car, drink a certain beverage, or wear a certain brand of clothes. These messages have an impact.

I am in the television business, and I am constantly amazed how our industry underestimates the intelligence of the viewing audience. The average young person, upon their graduation from high school, has witnessed thousands of murders and violent crimes via the television. The television industry would have you believe that this has no impact on them as "they understand the difference between fiction and reality." On the other hand, these same television executives will justify charging you well in excess of $1 million for one minute of air time during the Super Bowl to sell your latest breakfast cereal.

The single characteristic shared by more top executives is the fact that they read or listen to positive, motivational, affirming material on a regular basis.

We must understand that we are in a battle of cost and value, and it is a battle for the mind. If we truly are a product of what we think about all day, the most valuable property we can ever own would be a positive, self-affirming thought.

In a recent survey of the top executives of the Fortune 500 companies, it was determined that the characteristic that these business leaders have most in common is not their education, skill level, or work ethic. It was discovered that the single characteristic shared by more top executives is the fact that they read or listen to positive, motivational, affirming material on a regular basis.

The next time you have the choice between feeding your ego, feeding your body, or feeding your mind, try feeding your mind and you will find that it will result in a permanent change that will be manifested in every area of your life.

Today's the day!

MAKING MONEY VS. EARNING MONEY

THERE HAS NEVER BEEN A MONEY SHORTAGE. THERE IS, FROM TIME TO time, an idea, inspiration, motivation, or creativity shortage. This shortage may manifest itself in the lack of money. It's important to realize that the only people who make money work at the mint. Everyone else earns money.

There is a fair exchange between what an individual does and what he is paid for completing that task. The pay for a task increases as its degree of difficulty, danger, expertise, or the amount of training required increases. There are many jobs that you could be trained to do and be in a position to accomplish the required task by the end of the first day. In most cases, these jobs do not pay particularly well. On the other hand, if you wish to be a neurosurgeon—while you will not be performing the task by the end of the first day—at the point you have completed many years of training, you will be compensated very well.

It is important to realize that there are certain humanitarian and service-oriented positions where the compensation is, at least in part, in the satisfaction received in completing the task. For example, members of the clergy and most notably here in Oklahoma, public school teachers. I think we would all agree that their importance and amount of responsibility they take on, far exceeds their monetary compensation.

The next time you hear yourself say, "I would like to make more money," simply ask yourself the question, "What am I willing to do to create more value in the products and services I provide to the people around me?" Once you have answered this question and you begin working to that level, your earnings will most certainly follow.

I wish you all of the money that you are willing to earn.

Today's the day!

TIME AND MONEY

WE'VE ALL HEARD THE TIMEWORN ADAGE THAT TIME IS MONEY. LIKE most timeworn adages, this one—at its center—has a real practical truth for all of us. Most of us go to work each day and spend eight-to-ten hours or more in exchange for a paycheck. While many of us enjoy our jobs, if we are honest or even practical, we will admit that we are exchanging our time for someone else's money. This makes sense to us in the professional area of our lives, but too many of us miss the time-and-money equation as it relates to our personal lives.

I know top-level executives who come home after a long day at work and spend their evening doing yard work or household chores instead of spending time with their family or other recreational pursuits they might enjoy. If you like doing yard work or housework, this doesn't apply to you, but we must realize when we are performing any task, the time-and-money principles still apply.

While we are doing that yard work, we are exchanging quality family time or personal recreation time for the price of hiring the teenager down the block. In a perfect time-and-money equation, you should spend your time doing what you do best, and what creates the most value, and results in the most money. Then you should hire people to do the other things that they do well, leaving you free to pursue other areas of life.

The same thing that has made our civilization progress over the centuries will make our personal lives rich and diverse. When people are free to do what they do best, while allowing others to do the necessary tasks of life, we make progress—culturally and personally.

Think about your life and your schedule. What do you enjoy doing most, and what creates the most value? Do those things, and use some of your money to invest in buying back more time. In the final analysis, time is all we have.

Today's the day!

WHAT DO YOU KNOW NOW?

HAVE YOU EVER CAUGHT YOURSELF OR SOMEONE ELSE SAYING, "IF I had only known then what I know now…"?

All of us, at one time or another, have realized that sometime in the past, we were in possession of some very valuable information; but we may not have known it was valuable information at the time. Whether it was the hot new stock that we could have bought for a song several years ago or the cheap land right across the street from the newest mega shopping mall, hindsight is always 20/20.

Everything makes sense and is totally clear in retrospect; however, you can't drive through life while looking in the rearview mirror. While the view in the rearview mirror may be perfect, the result will inevitably be disastrous. No matter how frightening, murky, or uncertain, we have to make our decisions and live our lives in the future.

> *Genius is often simply a matter of looking at things*
> *a little bit differently than the rest of the world.*

If we can accept the fact that many times in our lives we have been in possession of extremely valuable information whether we knew it or not, we can also accept the fact that we are, right now, in possession of some very valuable information that may be unbelievably profitable or beneficial in the near future. You will either take advantage of this knowledge now or someday you will look back on today with the proverbial statement, "If I had only known then what I know now…."

Tomorrow's "then" is today's "right now." The question is not whether you do or don't have the information. The question is, can you recognize it and act upon it? Wisdom and leadership come from recognizing, anticipating, and acting on facts and details that others overlook.

Genius is often simply a matter of looking at things a little bit differently than the rest of the world, or simply recognizing that there are many treasures all around us that are available to anyone who will recognize them. Don't wait until it's too late to recognize your treasures. Look, listen, and act.

Today's the day!

THE U.S. OPEN COMES TO A CLOSE

MILLIONS OF PEOPLE AROUND THE WORLD SPENT THE MIDDLE PART of June totally focused on the U.S. Open Golf Tournament. As the various stories unfolded, there were many lessons to be learned. People who thought that Tiger Woods was unbeatable learned that, while he may be the best in the world at what he does, no one is ever invincible.

Thousands who were present and millions watching on TV saw three elite, professional golfers at the top of their game miss short putts on the final hole that would have won the tournament. I have heard many people in the media and in person say, "I could have made any of those three putts." In reality, if you took away the pressure, the tension, and everything that was at stake, any of us probably could have made those putts. But life doesn't work that way.

Those three players each made in excess of 275 shots during the week that virtually no one else in the world could have made. Their high level of skill brought them to the last hole on the last day where they each missed the most simple shot of the week. This points out the old adage "You're only as strong as your weakest link."

Often in business and in life, it is the little, mundane details that are overlooked which cause us to experience a poor performance. Think of the people you know or the companies you do business with that impress you. Chances are, if you'll really explore what makes the difference, it is the little things. A courteous greeting, a polite thank you note, or simply going the extra mile as a normal course of business could make all the difference.

Many of us fly with the airlines as a normal part of our routine. Travelers often speak of good flights and bad flights. If you ask them to define the difference, generally it will come down to a warm smile, a polite greeting, or a standard of professionalism just slightly above average. As you go through your day today, remember that the big things are important and they are what we focus on, but quite often, like the three golfers in the U.S. Open, you will be remembered for and live and die based on the little things.

Today's the day!

PERSISTENCE PAYS OFF

SUCCESS IN LIFE, BE IT PERSONAL OR PROFESSIONAL, COMES FROM PER-forming at a high level for an extended period of time. Hap Lowry is a friend and colleague on the professional speaking platform. He has a number of powerful statements he calls "Hapisms." One of my favorites is "Persistence pays high dividends both professionally and personally."

We all know people who had a great idea and simply quit before the goal line. There are others who, due to an extraordinary performance one time, reached their goal but do not perform at a persistently high level so that their brief success simply fades into the mist of oblivion. They become the actors, authors, singers, business people who, whenever their name is mentioned, someone will ask the eternal question, "What-ever happened to them?" Life comes down to performing at a high level over a long period of time instead of outstanding performances just once or twice.

> *Success in life, be it personal or professional,*
> *comes from performing at a high level*
> *for an extended period of time.*

Two years ago, I began my own personal exercise and eating revolu-tion. My new lifestyle has resulted in weight loss of over 100 pounds and an improved physical condition that I would have not thought possible for someone who has already celebrated his fortieth birthday. I discov-ered that persistence and consistency is the key to ongoing success. From time to time, people will come into the fitness facility where I exercise, and they will work out at a superhuman pace for one or two days, and then they go away, never to be heard from again.

I have been reviewing leadership surveys conducted to determine the elements that top performing executives use to evaluate themselves. They ask questions like: "Am I on target for my goals?" "Are the people around me dedicated to our collective success?" And many others. One of the most intriguing questions to come out of the executive surveys is the following: "Is my pace sustainable?" If your pace is not sustainable, you will most likely never see the mountaintop, and if you do, it will only be for a brief moment before you slide back down the mountainside, losing the progress you have made.

Today, as you look at your long term goals and your short term tasks, part of making sure you are on target is to know that the things you are doing today will lead you to your ultimate destiny, and that today's performance is repeatable and sustainable. Dedicate yourself to a consistent performance that will be both reliable and dependable. The race does not always go to the swiftest. It goes to the individual who realizes that today is simply one more rung on the ladder toward your goal.

Today's the day!

DO OR DON'T PENDING LIST

AS A BLIND PERSON IN A PRINT AND PAPER WORLD, I HAVE LEARNED several lessons that I think can benefit us all. Since I have people read all of my mail and other printed material, I have formulated a policy over the years. That is, to handle all paperwork only once.

Initially, this started as a means to maximize the time and effort of those whose eyes I use to decipher printed documents. I have discovered that this policy is even more effective in creating efficiency and priorities in my life.

Too many people waste effort and energy while creating anxiety by not dealing with things immediately. When I am confronted with a matter demanding attention, I have three choices. One: Do it now. Two: Don't do it at all. Or three: Put it on a pending list to be reviewed at a later date. While this seems elementary, it has revolutionized my business life. Each day, I simply follow my list of priorities and put any new projects I encounter into one of the three categories previously mentioned. In our lives, the truly important too-often takes a back seat to the immediate or the urgent.

Take a look at your "to do" list and ask yourself these questions with respect to each of the items, "What is the worst thing that would happen if I don't do this at all?" Then ask, "What is the best thing that could happen if I do this?" And finally ask, "Can this be just as effective if I do it later?"

I do not believe in procrastinating, but I do believe in prioritizing. Too often, we eliminate important things from our schedule, replacing it with tasks that could be done later or not at all.

We all spend a lot of time studying the best way to invest our money. Unfortunately, very little emphasis is placed on how we invest our most important and irreplaceable commodity: our time.

Today's the day!

PROBLEMS AND PRIORITIES

EVERY DAY, WE ARE ALL FACED WITH TWO IMPORTANT QUESTIONS that greatly impact our productivity. These two questions are what are we doing? And how well are we doing it? Most of the emphasis in human behavior and personal development deals with the second question how well are we doing it? Very seldom do the success gurus focus on the primary element which is what are we doing?

Please understand that you can be doing a great job of accomplishing the wrong thing. It's like the maintenance man on the Titanic who was cleaning the deck as the ship was slowly sinking. Cleaning the deck can certainly be an important thing, but while the ship is sinking, it does not even approach a priority.

I had the opportunity to speak to my accountant a number of times prior to the tax deadline. In his utter frustration with some of his clients, he had adopted a new motto that says, "Your current crisis brought on by your poor planning is not my immediate problem."

We are only as big as the smallest thing that it takes to divert us from our destination.

Each day, there are a number of people who are determined to make their problems your priorities. We have all had the experience of being at our desk involved in very productive and fruitful activities when someone calls to interrupt us. The classic example is, of course, the sales call. Telephone sales people make their living from calling prospects on the telephone. However, it is certainly not your priority during the productive part of your workday to be bothered with these kinds of calls.

Focus on your personal and professional mission statement, then ask yourself, "What are the things I can do today that will get me from here to there?" These activities become your priorities. Anything less important that diverts you from your priority is a problem. Remember, we are only as big as the smallest thing that it takes to divert us from our destination.

Oftentimes, the more productive things on our daily schedule are not the easiest things for us to accomplish. Therefore, we allow or even welcome intrusions and interruptions that sabotage our productivity. At the end of the day, you will either be one day closer to or farther from your goal.

Make today count.

Today's the day!

INVESTING IN YOUR FUTURE

THERE HAS BEEN A GREAT DEAL IN THE MEDIA RECENTLY ABOUT THE stock market and the economy. Although I started my career in business as an investment broker and member of the New York Stock Exchange, the only advice I can give you about the market is that it has been up and down in the past, and this will continue into the future. Beware of anyone with easy answers to complex questions.

In the final analysis, there are only three areas in which you can spend or invest your money. First, you can buy things. Second, you can buy security. And, third, you can buy memories. As in most things, there is no simple right or wrong answer. This is not a "one size fits all" proposition; however, I would like to explore the benefits and pitfalls of each of the three investment areas.

If you invest in things properly, you will discover that new clothes, cars, homes, etc. are very nice but will not make you happy at the end of the day. These are tools that can help you live a lifestyle that you have chosen for yourself. As long as you control these things and they don't control you, you will be fine.

If you invest too heavily in security, you may find that you are totally prepared for the proverbial "rainy day" and you may experience a long-term drought. An umbrella is a nice thing to have during a downpour, but if you own seven of them, it is really too much no matter what the weather. Be prepared for tomorrow, but don't sacrifice today.

Finally, you can invest in memories. I've heard it said that we don't remember years as much as we remember the moments. Investing in those magic moments can reap tremendous dividends in your own personal success and happiness.

Seek the level of investment in each of these three areas that will give you the returns you desire. Today, determine to focus on your resources and how you invest them in these three areas. Find the strategy that is right for you and stick with it, come rain or come shine.

Today's the day!

Who's In Charge?

In our day-to-day lives, control is often an illusion. There are many books about time management, but—when it's all said and done—we can't manage time. We can only hope to manage ourselves.

A co-worker of mine is undergoing the experience of having a new baby at her house. She commented to me, "It's amazing how this little six-pound person, who is totally helpless, can take over everyone's lives." Whether or not you have had the experience of having a new baby at your house, I know that you have had the experience of having someone else control your time, your day, and ultimately your life.

Those of you who are regular readers of *Winners' Wisdom* know that we spend a lot of time talking about taking control of your thoughts, goals, and destiny. This is only possible when we control our days, hours, and minutes. Many times, we start our day with the best of intentions to accomplish the tasks that will result in moving us toward our goal; but then, inevitably, the phone rings, someone comes into our office, or any one of a million things jumps up and distracts us.

Often these distractions cannot be avoided. Success lies in how quickly we can get back on the right track.

> *Minutes, hours, and days are all that you have to invest in making your future what you want it to be. Invest them wisely.*

If you are starting out on an automobile trip of 1,000 miles, you can have every detail planned, all of your stops precisely scheduled, and have every minute factor considered; however, something as simple as a rusty nail on the road anywhere along your 1,000-mile route can give you a flat tire and totally disrupt your plans. Your trip is not a failure unless you allow that disruption to side-track you from your goal or to affect your attitude. We must have our goals set in concrete, but the methods and routes must be flexible.

When you finally reach the mountaintop, those around you will not ask you, "How did you get here?" They will simply applaud the fact that you did.

Minutes, hours, and days are all that you have to invest in making your future what you want it to be. Invest them wisely.

Today's the day!

PROTECTING PERSONAL PRIORITIES

WHETHER YOU ARE A TOP LEVEL CORPORATE EXECUTIVE, A HOME-maker, a student, or an individual enjoying retirement years, you probably begin each day with a list of things to do. People who do not have a list of daily, weekly, monthly, or annual tasks quite simply baffle me. Either they have a photographic mind, or they are doing very little in their life, or they have a lot of priority items falling through the pro-verbial cracks. In any event, if we are going to maximize our time, effort, and energy—which in the final analysis is about all we have—we need to establish our priorities, and then we need to protect those priorities.

Every individual needs what I call a personal mission statement. This is what defines who you are and what is important to you in your life. Each of your daily activities must be valued in light of your personal mission statement. We all have the necessary maintenance things that must be done. We have to get our oil changed, get our hair cut, and visit the dentist. These things must work in and around the priorities in our life.

The most productive people I know have no less than four or five priorities in a day and no more than 15 to 20. On a normal day, if you only have one or two things you're working on, you need to reexamine your priorities or mission statement. If your average day has more than 20 things you have to get done, directly relating to your job or mis-sion in life, you may need to look at delegating or combining some of these tasks.

If you have a high number of daily activities, you at least must prioritize them. This can be done by quickly answering the follow-ing questions.

1. If I could only get one thing done today, which one would it be?

2. Is there anyone else who can be doing this other than me?

3. What if this particular item is not done today?

4. What if this particular item is not done at all?

5. Which of my priorities will put me in the best position to get where I want to be tomorrow, next week, next year, etc.?

You must have your priorities firmly established in your mind because, throughout your day, you will run into any number of people who, for whatever reason, have you listed on their priority list. They may be a salesman trying to sell you something, an old friend wanting to reconnect with you, a neighbor or colleague wanting to visit or network, along with any number of other activities in which people want you to engage.

Keep in mind that even valid activities may not be your priorities. If something comes up during the day that is obviously someone else's priority, it needs to be ranked in your priority list before you can change your plan of action. As you go through your day today, remember—if it's worth doing, it's worth prioritizing.

Today's the day!

Time is Not Money

I've heard it said my whole life that "Time is Money." Certainly I understand, in the context of maximizing efficiency on the job, this can be true. But in reality, time is time and money is money. Try going to the grocery store and when they ring up your total tell them you don't have any money but you're willing to spend some time in the store. Or when you have a deadline on a project and you run out of time, you'll find out that offering them money may not solve the problem.

We each have 1,440 minutes in a day. We choose how we invest each of these minutes. I understand that you have commitments at jobs, schools, and other appointments, but when you really analyze it, you control your own time, and you simply made these commitments.

It's amazing to me how we confuse time and money and often waste one while we value another. For example, if someone came into your office during your most productive time of the day and interrupted you with a long, detailed description of something that really doesn't matter to you, would you protect your investment of time and ask them politely to leave or to come back later? Unfortunately, too often we allow people to waste our productive time. On the other hand, if you have several twenty dollar bills in your desk and someone comes in and grabs one and begins to walk out, you will probably say something. While we invariably wouldn't think of letting someone steal our money, we routinely let people steal our time. In reality, the time that individual stole from your workday is obviously worth much more than the $20 they took.

We each have 1,440 precious minutes throughout the day. We can allocate them to work, play, family time, self-improvement, reflection, study, or relaxation. Each of us has to decide how to prioritize our time.

Unfortunately, we often give other people control of our most precious irreplaceable asset which is the minutes we have to invest throughout each day of our lives.

There is no free time. If someone wastes your time at work, you may say to yourself, "I'll just finish this later," which invariably moves all your projects during the day to a later time. This causes you to work late or move part of today's activities to tomorrow. Unfortunately, we don't see that this person wasting our work time caused our work time to back up into our family time causing our family time to back up into our personal development time and on and on. That wasted time can never be retrieved.

Certainly having small talk with co-workers or playing a mindless game or even simply allowing your mind and body to relax can all be good utilizations or investments of your 1,440 minutes each day. Just don't let anyone else make those decisions.

As you go through your day today, be sure to spend your time and your money wisely.

Today's the day!

Good vs. Best

It is better to do the right thing adequately than the wrong thing well. All of us from time to time feel the temptation to focus our efforts on things that come easy to us, come quickly to us, or bring us the attention we seek. This short term approach rarely brings long term success.

We live in a microwave society. We want everything easier, faster, and more convenient. Unfortunately, success is rarely prepared in a microwave. It is more of a crock pot process. We've all heard the stories of the "overnight sensation" that, at further examination, was the culmination of years and decades of effort.

If you have ever watched or coached Little League sports, you will readily notice a phenomenon. The best hitters want to practice batting while the best fielders want to practice catching and the best pitchers want to practice throwing. Little Leaguers, as well as you and I, want to spend our time doing the things we do best. Unfortunately, often our performance is relegated to our weakest link. If you wanted to become an airline pilot because you loved the process of taxiing and taking off in an airplane but you did not enjoy landing, you would have very little success. There is no such thing as a good flight that ends in a bad landing.

We may become known for the things we do best. We become successful for performing everything competently. We all want to be specialists. Unfortunately, particularly when we start out, we need to be generalists. Few people ever get the luxury of only focusing on one task. Long term success, wealth, and happiness are built from consistency. An 80 per cent or 90 per cent effort may not succeed. If your favorite restaurant served your entree perfect every time, exactly as you like it, but they burned the bread, forgot the salad, spilled your drink, and ignored your requests for service, it would not long be your favorite restaurant. In most areas of life, you have to perform a multitude of tasks adequately in order to succeed.

If you will objectively examine your personal and professional life, you will notice a number of facets. Each of these facets is equally important to the extent that success is not possible without them. If you succeed in your financial life but ruin your health, you have failed. If you remain healthy but cannot pay your bills and afford the necessities, you have failed. If you have an outstanding career but lose your family, you have failed.

As you go through your day today, continue to excel at the things you do best, but focus your effort and energy on those things you want to do better.

Today's the day!

Hidden in Plain Sight

OFTENTIMES, THE GREAT DEVELOPMENTS IN LIFE AND IN BUSINESS come not from obscure technological breakthroughs. Instead, they come from something standing right in front of us, staring us in the face. The whole world is looking for a great idea.

The only thing you have to do to have a great idea is to go through your daily personal and professional tasks and wait for something bad to happen. Then ask yourself the magic question: "How could I have avoided that?" The answer to that question is a great idea. The only thing you have to do to create a great business opportunity is to, once again, wait for something bad to happen and ask yourself the more all-encompassing question, "How could I help other people avoid that problem?" The answer to this question may well be a million dollar business idea.

Often when we hear about or read about a tremendously profitable breakthrough in business, marketing, or industry, our first thought is not "How in the world could anybody ever think of that?" More often our reaction is, "Why didn't I think of that?" Too often the reason you and I don't think of that is not because we don't have the same facts and details. It's simply because we weren't looking at the information in front of us creatively, and we weren't thinking about what could be instead of what is.

Business, and life in general, is a balancing act between excelling in the current systems while creating new and improved ways of doing things and meeting the needs of those around us. There was a time when building a better covered wagon was a profitable, meaningful pursuit; however 150 years later, it would be laughable to still be trying to build a great covered wagon. On the other hand, if you'd been building covered wagons in the 1850s, it would be just as absurd to spend all of your time drawing and designing jet airplanes that could not possibly be a part of your short term or even long term reality.

> *Make today great with what you have*
> *before you while making tomorrow even*
> *better with that which is yet to come.*

We all know people who are so focused on the future they miss the present. It is equally sad to think of people who are so focused on the present they miss the future.

As you go through your day today, do everything in your power to juggle the two challenges of making today great with what you have before you while making tomorrow even better with that which is yet to come.

Today's the day!

Priorities and Possibilities

In the final analysis, the only thing you and I have to invest in either our personal or professional lives is our time. Money and resources can come and go. They can also be replaced. Time is the absolute irreplaceable commodity that we all deal with. We all have the same 24 hours a day to invest; therefore, people who succeed in life on their own terms are those who have learned to become great investors of their time, effort, and energy.

Like most things in life, being a great investor of time is not a black and white matter. Instead, there are a number of variables impacting how you should utilize your most precious asset. I divide the two extremes of time management into priorities and possibilities.

Priorities are the day to day mundane things that must be done. These priorities would include paying your bills, answering your correspondence, returning phone calls, etc. While these things may not get you where you want to go, they are important because they keep you where you are.

On the other hand, possibilities are the big picture, long range, creative pursuits that outline our potential greatness. It is critical that you invest some of your time resources in this area; however, if you invest too much in this one category, you will be like the ship's captain who is looking at the far horizon with his telescope while he is hitting an iceberg directly in front of him. Conversely, if he only worries about missing the icebergs, he could safely wander around in circles for years.

Most of us are very organized with our priorities and relegate our possibilities to any time we may have left over at the end of the day, week, or month. I recommend that, for scheduling purposes only, you make your possibilities a priority on your daily list of things to do. Block out periods of time to consider new marketing ideas, long term business strategies, great travel or vacation plans, etc. Your possibilities deserve more than whatever time you may have left over, but if you don't handle your priorities, you may find yourself out of business and out of luck.

As you go through your day today, find and document a balance between priorities and possibilities. Realize that it doesn't benefit you to work today unless you have a future, but you have no future unless you handle priorities today.

And, as always, *today's the day!*

NOT A PERFECT WORLD

MANY DISCUSSIONS, LECTURES, AND COMMENTARIES FOR CENTURIES have started with the phrase, "In a perfect world." This denotes that if the world were perfect, we would do everything, be everything, create everything, and fix everything. As wonderful as this is to think about, we all have to realize and live with the fact that it's simply not a perfect world. This is not a negative or pessimistic viewpoint, but a realistic one.

I am among the most optimistic, upbeat, and encouraging people you will ever meet regarding the positive state of the world today and how much better I believe tomorrow will be; but even with my perspective, I have to admit that the world is far from perfect. This means we are forced to make choices.

Each day, we are bombarded with a myriad of opportunities to invest our time, effort, energy, and money. Additionally, we are asked to donate our efforts and resources to numerous causes. We are implored to spend 30 minutes here, an hour there, and 10 minutes each morning doing something. If you added up all the suggestions for our time and money, we would earn billions, donate millions, and utilize hundreds of hours each day. This is simply not possible, and the weight of all these decisions can make us far less effective in our personal and professional lives.

Here are some rules for deciding how to invest your time, effort, energy, resources, and donations.

1. Make sure it matters more to you than to anyone else. Oftentimes, we are pursuing the passion of a salesman or a fundraiser instead of our own wants, needs, and desires.

2. Be sure that the course you are pursuing is the most efficient and effective. All of your resources are limited, so you've got

to use them wisely to get from where you are to where you
want to be.

3. Learn how to say, "No." This innocent-seeming two-letter
   word stands between you and peace, prosperity, and happiness. If you are going to say, "Yes," to a few priorities about
   which you are passionate, you are going to have to say, "No,"
   to everything else.

We live in a world where we do not have to settle for average or even
good. We can deal exclusively with things, people, and situations that
are great. It's not a perfect world, so we can't do everything. Once we
realize this, we simply need to make sure we are doing the right things.

As you go through your day today, realize that in a perfect world
we would do everything. Since the world is not perfect, we will do the
perfect things for our world.

Today's the day!

COMSTOCK GOLD

RECENTLY, I WAS READING A HISTORIC NOVEL ABOUT THE GOLD RUSH in California and Nevada in the mid-1800s. It was fascinating to learn how people lived during that time and in that place. There are a multitude of lessons to be learned in observing any situation.

The early miners struck some promising looking veins of gold, and the Gold Rush was on. People came from around the world with nothing more than their hopes and dreams of gold. As the various mines developed, it became much more expensive and labor intensive to get the ore out of the ground. Many people who came halfway around the world expecting to get rich, only got a job working in someone else's mine.

These West Coast mines were unique in that there was blue clay that continued to seep into each of the tunnels and mine shafts. They had to assign many workers to do nothing more than scoop up this clay and haul it out of the mine, creating large mountains of this waste blue clay material. This clay removal made the mining process more dangerous and more expensive.

They called in mining experts from around the world to determine how to stop this blue clay from creeping into the mine works. One deep mine expert arrived from Ireland and, as he was walking up the hill to the mine shaft, he noticed the enormous pile of blue clay. He casually commented, "That is the largest pile of silver ore I've ever seen."

As the gold played out, the Comstock Lode became one of the richest deposits of silver the world has ever known. Many fortunes were built in just a few short years—not because of gold, but because of a waste byproduct they had overlooked.

Oftentimes, wisdom and genius come from simply observing your current situation from another angle.

Unless you and I are interested in silver mines, this may not have any direct application to our lives; however, it may be worth more than the silver or the gold if we will come to understand the significance. We must ask ourselves the golden question: What opportunities are we overlooking simply because we think we should be working in another direction? Success generally lies in recognizing and exploiting value before anyone else does. You may already have the key to everything you want in your hands. Step back and look at it from a different perspective. Don't only think about what you see, but think about what other people might see. Oftentimes, wisdom and genius come from simply observing your current situation from another angle.

As you go through your day today, look past the gold and even the silver. You may already possess more than you think.

Today's the day!

WEALTH 101

YESTERDAY I HEARD A STATISTIC THAT IS TREMENDOUSLY SIGNIFI-
cant. The first impression of this statistic was so insignificant that I
almost didn't get it. Then the true import of what I was hearing dawned
on me. Last month, the national average savings rate was a negative 1%.
At first glance, 1% doesn't seem like a big number, and the fact that
it only deals with the savings rate doesn't seem to indicate an immediate crisis; however, there are some facts in play here that we need
to understand.

Interest rates are still at a historic low that most of us have not experienced in our lifetimes. Our economy is relatively healthy and growing
at a good pace. Employment is approaching a level we would consider
full employment. And, overall, the economic outlook is pretty good.
The last time we had a negative 1% savings rate nationally, was in 1933.
This, our fans of history will remember, was the low point of the Great
Depression; therefore, this begs the question: "What's going to happen
if things get really bad?"

This is probably a good point for you and me to review the myths
and realities of wealth building. The greatest myth about wealthy people
is that they either inherited the money or won the lottery. In reality,
over 90% of millionaires are first generation millionaires who earned,
saved, and invested their own money. People who win the lottery are
more likely to file bankruptcy in the following 10 years than the average
working class person in our society. Therefore, with respect to wealth
building, we must rely on the old adage: "If it is to be, it is up to me."

Now that we've dispelled the myths and established personal responsibility, let's go over a few rules for building our wealth.

1. Spend less than you earn.

2. Avoid borrowing money.

3. Live on a budget.

4. Save and invest regularly.

This would seem to be an elementary school explanation of wealth building. In reality, many millionaires in our society only have an elementary school education. If you're going to win any game, you first need to understand the rules. Then follow the lead of those who have already won. Whether I am writing books, speaking from the platform, or putting together these weekly columns, probably my best advice ever is, "Don't take advice from anybody that doesn't have what you want." This certainly applies as you strive to reach your financial goals.

As you go through your day today, remember the simple rules of wealth building and apply them to your life. They are, indeed, simple but not easy. If it were easy, everyone would be rich.

Today's the day!

WINNING THE LOTTERY

THESE WEEKLY COLUMNS—THANKS TO PEOPLE LIKE YOU—ARE included in numerous newspapers, magazines, and online publications, read by people, literally, all around the world. I mention this here because today's topic begins with a somewhat local reference.

Recently, my home state of Oklahoma has begun a lottery. Oklahomans now have an opportunity not only to participate in our state lottery but to buy a ticket in the national Power Ball lottery. The TV, radio, and newspaper ads inform us that there are literally millions up for grabs.

Well-meaning and good people in my home state and elsewhere will continue to debate whether a lottery is good or bad. I will leave this debate to them; however, I will pose a simple question to those of you who regularly purchase multiple lottery tickets. I'm assured by national statistics that there are many people who buy hundreds of dollars' worth of lottery tickets each week. Let's assume that you only buy $40 worth of lottery tickets each week throughout your working life. If I were to ask the population of lottery ticket buyers if they would be pleased if they bought their tickets regularly for all those years knowing that at some point they were guaranteed to win $1 million, the answer would be a resounding YES.

In reality, the odds of winning $1 million in the lottery, even buying all those tickets over all those years, is something less than the odds of getting struck by lightning. On the other hand, if these same individuals were to put their $40 a week in the average growth stock mutual fund over their working lives, they would historically be guaranteed to have well over $1 million had they done this over any period in the last 50 years.

Once I came to the realization of these startling statistics, contrasting the lottery vs. conservative and consistent investing, I shared my new found wisdom with several people who buy lottery tickets. You may or may not be as shocked as I was to know that they are still buying their lottery tickets and have yet to open their mutual fund account. This confirms something I have believed for years. That is, if you divided all the money up equally among all of us, within a few short years the money would find its way back to the people who have it now. The rich get richer, and the poor get poorer for the simple reason that money is not a cause, it is an effect. Wealth or lack thereof is a symptom of other factors in our lives.

As you go through your day today, look for opportunities to avoid long shots, and invest your future in a sure thing.

Today's the day!

Partnering Possibilities

FORMING PARTNERSHIPS CAN EITHER BE THE BEST OF TIMES OR THE worst of times. There is very little middle ground when it comes to creating or dealing with partners. People who have experienced partnerships will either tell you it's the best thing they ever did or the worst mistake they ever made.

People often form partnerships for the wrong reasons. Avoid partnerships if any of the following resembles your reason for wanting to form a relationship.

1. You think it would be fun or interesting to have a partner in business with you.

2. You're afraid it may be lonely or boring to go it alone.

3. You believe your potential partner is going to do all the things you don't want to do.

4. You believe your partner is going to bring a lot of business to the endeavor.

5. You have a talented friend who is out of work.

All of these may be important elements as you consider a business relationship, but always remember that individuals can be vendors, customers, contractors, consultants, and participants in a joint venture without entering into a permanent partnership. People who rush into partnerships are like a couple who decides to get married on the first date. It may seem like a good idea, but rarely will it prove to be positive. In order to be even contemplated, a partnership must have the following elements.

1. All partners have clearly identified talents, assets, and responsibilities that they are bringing to the partnership.

2. All partners have very clear expectations of responsibilities, workloads, and chain of command.

3. There is a very clear and written partnership agreement for every possible contingency.

4. There is a very clear and understandable exit strategy.

Partnerships are generally formed when spirits are high and prospective partners are optimistic. This is the easiest time to discuss how to handle potential problems. As good as you may feel now, it is important to realize that your partner may disagree with you, your partner may lose interest, your partner may become disabled, your partner may go through a divorce, or your partner may die. Each of these possibilities and a myriad of others must be considered. When you are in a relationship with the right partners, there is nothing better. One plus one can equal 100 or even 1,000 if you are with the right partner.

As you go through your day today, make sure any partnership you consider offers you the best of times, not the worst of times.

Today's the day!

NET WORTH VS. NET VALUE

MOST PEOPLE IN OUR SOCIETY HAVE EXTREMELY VAGUE OR GENERAL financial goals. These goals, in some capacity, surround the word "more." These people want more money, more savings, more income, more investments, more retirement, and more stuff. We have become a consumer society. We are bombarded moment to moment by advertisements, commercials, and countless messages telling us that "You are your stuff." The implication is if you had more you would be more.

Most people are, at some level, unhappy. The consumer messages tell us that the people who have more than we do are happy; therefore, we simply need to get more things in our lives. As someone who has been relatively poor and now relatively rich in my life, I can echo the old adage that "All things being equal, rich is better." But it is important to note that neither money, nor the things that money will buy, make us happy. Happiness is an internal thermostat that we set ourselves. Abraham Lincoln, someone who was plagued his whole life with clinical depression, said, "People are about as happy as they decide to be."

Most people are running faster and pushing harder to get more. Too often, they are performing a job they don't enjoy for people they don't respect to get things to impress others who simply don't care. If you were to probe these striving individuals in search of more, at some point they would tell you they are doing this for their family. Let's examine your net worth vs. your net value as it relates to your family.

1. Think of the people in your ancestry who have impacted your life and the way you live the most. You will probably discover these high-impact people left you life values instead of money.

2. Think of the people in your past who impacted you during your formative years. You will likely determine that they invested time, love, and lessons into your life and not just capital.

3. Think of the special times with friends and family that meant the most to you then and now. You will probably realize that these occasions may have been low-cost or no-cost events.

4. What are you leaving to your heirs in the way of time, lessons, and memories? If you're trading these things in for the pursuit of more, you may be spending the most valuable part of their inheritance without their permission. They want you, not just your money.

Like most life lessons, this one is a balancing act. We human beings seek black-and-white answers to gray questions. Nothing will replace money in the things that money does, but beyond that point, nothing will replace you in the hearts, minds, and spirits of the special people in your life.

As you go through your day today, find ways to increase both your net worth and your net value for those you love.

Today's the day!

EVERY SHOT COUNTS

ALONG WITH MANY AMERICANS, I SPENT THIS PAST WEEKEND EXPLORing the outer limits of how much college basketball one person can really take in. With 65 teams going to the NCAA tournament and many conference championships, there was more college basketball than anyone can even imagine. As we listen to the commentary from the various network sportscasters, we all establish our favorites. A good announcer can really make the game come alive, and a bad one can really water down an otherwise exciting contest.

As often happens in hotly-contested basketball games, there were a number of times when victory and defeat seemed to be hanging in the balance and dependent upon the last shot. I heard any number of announcers emotionally intone, "It's all riding on this next shot. The game, the conference championship, and the whole season come down to this." While this seems to be true when a team is one point behind with 22 seconds to go, it really is not the case.

Several years ago, I had the privilege of appearing on a television show with the legendary UCLA basketball coach John Wooden. In that calm but confident demeanor that so many of us have come to respect, I remember him saying, "All baskets count for the same amount of points whether the shot is made in the first minute or the last minute of the game." I was struck by the profound impact of Coach Wooden's statement. That last-second shot that either signals victory or defeat is no more significant than the first shot of the game.

While this is true in a basketball game, it is even more true in our personal and professional lives. How often do we find ourselves rushing to meet a deadline with only hours or even a few minutes to spare? In that frantic last-minute commotion, we know that everything counts, and we can't waste any time. In reality, more times than not, if we had managed our time properly at the beginning of a task, the last few hours would not be critical because we would have already completed the task, had an opportunity to double check our work, and go on to the next opportunity before us.

Life will present us with enough crisis situations without our manufacturing more of them by mismanaging our time and resources. Whether it is in life or a basketball game, we should strive to have already won the contest long before it comes down to a last-second frantic shot.

Today's the day!

Smart vs. Intelligent

In our society, we have been sold a false premise for generations. This premise would tell us that the more we know, the more we earn, the more we're successful, and the happier we become. This is simply not true.

It has been said, "It's not how smart you are, but how you are smart." The world is full of people who might become Trivial Pursuit champions but simply don't know how to apply any knowledge in a form that brings them the results they seek. As a person who reads a book every day thanks to books on tape and a high speed tape player, I would be the first to say that education and learning are vital, but they are only vital when they can be applied to real world situations.

I have a good friend who is a surgeon. He makes a tremendous income practicing his profession. I remember him describing an operation to me. He said, "You simply make a cut and remove the damaged tissue." I told him I was shocked that he made thousands of dollars for making a simple incision. He responded, "For making the cut, I charge about $10. For knowing where to make the cut, I have become a millionaire."

In business and in life, it is often more important to understand the right question than to immediately have the answer. Now that we live in a world of high speed Internet access, knowledge rests at our fingertips. But knowing where to get the knowledge and how best to apply it to a real world problem or opportunity poses the same challenge it did to people who lived thousands of years ago.

In my career, I have sat for a number of tests to obtain professional licenses. Most of these tests were in the financial arena. Unfortunately, in order to become a broker, financial planner, or investment banker, you have to spend months learning how to master intricate financial calculations. It is sad that once you have passed your test, this knowledge is never used again, because these intricate financial calculations and many others are routinely done instantaneously at the touch of a computer key.

Someone could demonstrate amazing intelligence and unbelievable recall if they could memorize and recite a phone book. As incredible as this would be, it would turn out to be little more than a gimmick as all of the information in the phone book is readily available to anyone via computer, telephone, or by simply looking through their own phone book.

When you meet people who are successful or have achieved the things in life you want to achieve, get in the habit of asking them what knowledge they most often apply that brings them success. The answer may surprise you. Before you waste a lot of time learning the answers to questions no one is asking, determine what the real world solutions and answers are that people are seeking. The most valuable commodity on the planet is knowledge, but only if it is the right knowledge.

As you go through your day today, seek input and wisdom that will bring you toward the right knowledge.

Today's the day!

LABOR DAY 1955

THIS PAST WEEK, THERE WERE TWO SEPARATE AND DISTINCT DAYS when there were celebrations. These celebrations were not connected except in the way they came together in my mind. Labor Day was observed as it is each year. It may well be the least celebrated among all national holidays except for those actively involved in the labor movement. Unfortunately, most people look upon Labor Day as one last three-day holiday to end the summer.

The second day that was celebrated this past week was to commemorate the fact that my father has worked 50 years for the same organization and is still working today. As I have shared this milestone recently with a few friends and colleagues, they all seem to have a similar reaction. They are certain either I misstated the occasion or they somehow misunderstood. In reality, in August of 1955 after serving in the Navy, my father came to work for an organization in the mailroom, and he is still employed in that organization today. His service has taken him far beyond the mailroom as today he is President and Chief Executive Officer of a facility run by the organization where he began a half century ago.

Most people believe this kind of longevity and dedication within employment became extinct along with the dinosaurs if it ever, in fact, existed. My father represents a generation of people who looked at work differently. While they are concerned about their compensation, benefits, etc., my father's generation also looked at what they have to give and contribute to the organization and society as a whole.

My father looks at work as a calling, and he believes that if you treat your employer like you want your employer to treat you, it becomes the ultimate golden handcuff or parachute. Golden handcuffs and golden parachutes are terms that are used today in executive compensation. They are incentives to keep top level people or to make it easy for them to exit.

If you look at work like my father's generation, the employer doesn't have to produce any gimmicks to keep you, and you're not looking for an easy way out. Instead, employers value and honor the contribution made by longstanding associates, and these associates would no more leave their employer than they would leave their family. In fact, a good fit with respect to employment is more like a family for employer and employee than it is like a job. In these relationships, the questions of what you do, how well you do it, and who you serve are much more important than the standard "What's in it for me?" If you get the service right, everything's in it for you.

As you go through your day today, look for ways to create value in your workplace, and you will be rewarded far beyond your standard compensation.

Today's the day!

DON'T BET ON DEBT

WE HAVE BEEN BOMBARDED WITH ADVERTISING IMAGES AND MESsages to the extent that we hardly realize or notice. The late 20th and now the beginning of the 21st Centuries have brought us unprecedented consumer ads and have turned us all into Madison Avenue disciples. The reason corporations advertise is not because they like to spend billions of dollars. Instead, they advertise because they know it works.

Many people would be shocked to learn the number one item that is sold to us by all of these ad images and commercials is not cars, soft drinks, clothes, beer, or vacations. The number one thing you and I are confronted with via advertising is debt. Debt has become a high demand consumer item. It controls many people's budgets and a lot of people's lives.

Debt can be used as an effective tool, but this would be rare in comparison to the consumer debt utilization we experience in the 21st Century. There are a few times to consider debt and a high number of times to avoid it.

> *The number one thing you and I are confronted*
> *with via advertising is debt. Debt has*
> *become a high demand consumer item.*

You should consider debt when:

1. It is helping you buy a home, other real estate, or a property that is going up in value.

2. It helps you responsibly shift irregular expenses—e.g., making your holiday purchases in December but getting them paid for throughout the year.

3. If it is a realistic cushion for true emergencies. Debt can help you if you lose a job, have a health problem or other life crises.

Debt should be avoided in the following situations:

1. You are robbing Peter to pay Paul. In this instance, one credit card payment or utility bill is being shifted to another credit card payment or line of credit.

2. If you're buying things you don't want with money you don't have to impress people who don't care.

3. If you have more than half of your annual income in vehicle debt. It is foolish to pay interest to extend payments on things that are going down in value.

4. If you are living beyond your means while not planning for retirement, college education, and inevitable emergencies.

Like any other tool, debt can have a limited place. But in our society, it has become extremely prevalent. A hammer is a useful tool, but for the average homeowner, it may only be used a few times a year. If you hold a hammer in your hand all day every day, eventually everything will begin to look like a nail. The same thing happens when you have your credit card handy in the quick draw holster.

As you go through your day today, use debt on the rare occasions it serves you well, and avoid the advertising cries to get caught up in debt.

Today's the day!

4

SUCCESS IN ACTION

"Your goal, your dream, your sense of personal destiny, is your baby. Nobody will care for it, rescue it, or work for it like you will. Don't expect it of others. Do expect that kind of care and hard work on your part." —JIM STOVALL

SUCCESS IS VITALLY IMPORTANT BUT VIRTUALLY IMPOSSIBLE TO define. Success is not a direction, a speed, or an amount. It is, instead, the fulfillment of our deepest desires and greatest potential.

Individual success resembles a snowflake. Collectively, we can identify an accumulation of snow, but every flake is unique and an individual masterpiece.

We all strive for a definition of success, but we must be careful that the success we seek resembles our own definition. Our world is filled with people and countless media messages clamoring to define success for us. You and I must take on our own quest for success as a personal proposition that only we can define and only we can create.

REQUIRED READING FOR SUCCESS

I HAVE OFTEN HEARD IT SAID BY ONE OF THE GREAT LEADERS IN THE field of personal development, my friend Charlie "Tremendous" Jones, that five years from now you will be the same person that you are today with the exception of the people you meet and the books you read. I find that by reading books, we have the ability to meet the greatest minds in recorded history. They are simply waiting to give us the secrets of a successful life that have transcended the decades and centuries.

When I began my own personal quest for success, one of my mentors gave me a list of required reading material. He said, "No one can consider themselves well-read unless they have completed all ten of the books." Since then, my list has grown and shifted, but today, I want to give you my list of the ten books I believe that you would need to read in order to consider yourself well read in the areas of personal development and success.

1. *Think and Grow Rich* by Napoleon Hill
2. *The Magic of Thinking Big* by David J. Schwartz
3. *The Power of Positive Thinking* by Dr. Norman Vincent Peale
4. *Wake Up and Live* by Dorothea Brande
5. *The Psychology of Winning* by Dr. Denis Waitley
6. *How to Sell Anything to Anybody* by Joe Girard
7. *The 7 Habits of Highly Effective People* by Dr. Stephen Covey
8. *Tough Times Never Last, but Tough People Do* by Dr. Robert Schuller
9. *Giant Steps* by Tony Robbins
10. *Lead the Field* by Earl Nightingale

You may agree or disagree with my choices, and that really doesn't matter. What matters is, have you read your own list within the field of endeavor most important to your life goals?

People who study the history of the game of baseball are very busy debating who should be selected as the "all-century team." While some of the experts disagree, we can all understand that the list will be constantly changing. In a few years, some young player will emerge and have to be considered as one of the greatest of all times. In much the same way, your top ten list of books will be changing and growing for the rest of your life. And if you pursue your quest for the ultimate 10 books, you will continue to change and grow as well.

Today's the day!

THE SPIDER MONKEY SYNDROME

DESPITE MEDIA ACCOUNTS TO THE CONTRARY, WE LIVE AT THE BEST time, in the best place, in the middle of the best economy that the world has ever known. There will be more millionaires created this year than in any single year in recorded history. Given all of this prosperity, success, and opportunity, why do so many people fail to reach their goals? They, quite simply, fall victim to what I call the Spider Monkey Syndrome.

Spider monkeys are very small, approximately 4-6 inches tall, and look very much like humans. They live in the tallest trees in the most dense jungle in the Amazon basin. For years, people tried to capture spider monkeys but were unsuccessful, until one of the natives demonstrated the proper method.

To capture a spider monkey, you simply put one peanut inside of a small glass bottle, which you leave at the base of a tree. While you are gone, the spider monkey will climb down the tree, put his hand inside the bottle, and grab the peanut, making his fist too large to get out of the bottle. You have now captured a spider monkey. You can return and put a whole bag of peanuts right next to the spider monkey, and he will not let go of the one peanut he's holding onto that he can't eat and really didn't want in the first place. You can take away his freedom, you can even take his life, but he will not let go of the one peanut.

After exhaustive research on the subject of spider monkeys, I have come to the inescapable conclusion that spider monkeys are not very smart. But before we think too poorly of spider monkeys, we must ask ourselves: What is it in our lives we're holding onto that we really don't want or need that is keeping us from total success and our ultimate goal?

Failure and success cannot occupy the same space. You must let go of one to begin enjoying the other. Your destiny awaits.

Today's the day!

ASSUME YOU HAVE WHAT YOU NEED

THOSE OF YOU WHO SHARE MY PASSION FOR SIR ARTHUR CONAN Doyle's *Sherlock Holmes* books realize that the great detective always prevails, because he assumes that there is enough information to solve the mystery.

Too many of us are guilty of assuming that we don't have all of the pieces necessary to reach our goals. Complaints of "If I only had the education or time or contacts or money, etc." are often heard. Please understand that sometimes there are legitimate barriers between us and our success, but too often there are convenient challenges that masquerade as handy excuses for our remaining in the rut we find ourselves.

The story has been told of the graduate mathematics professor who was giving his doctoral candidates their final exam. In addition to the eight in-depth problems he gave his doctoral candidates as their final test, he threw them one last curve. The professor decided to give them an extra credit problem that was, in reality, one of the problems that Albert Einstein had never been able to solve, and it was assumed that this particular problem could and would never be solved.

To the doctoral professor's shock, three of his 20 students not only solved all eight of the regular problems, but accurately solved the extra credit problem as well. When he interviewed the three students who had solved Albert Einstein's "unsolvable problem," he asked them what it was that they had brought to the task that all of the greatest mathematicians in the world had failed to discover.

Finally, after a long silence, one of the students replied, "We were able to solve the problem because we assumed it was solvable. Everyone else had the built-in excuse that this problem could never be solved."

As you face the inevitable barriers on the way to reaching all of your goals, it is imperative that you differentiate between legitimate problems that must be solved or overcome and the built-in excuses we all give ourselves and those around us. Today, resolve to move toward your destiny assuming that everything you need you already have or you expect it to be provided for you at the point you need it most.

Today's the day!

THE WELL-WORN PATH TO SUCCESS

AS A FORMER NATIONAL CHAMPION OLYMPIC WEIGHTLIFTER, A SUCcessful author and speaker, and as the co-founder and president of the Emmy Award-winning Narrative Television Network, I am often asked: What is the key to success?

People seem to be particularly interested in my success because I am a blind person. The secret to my success is a very simple one. Follow the path of individuals who have already proven themselves to be successful.

While interviewing dozens of the most successful people from all walks of life for my book, *Success Secrets of Super Achievers*, I discovered they all have many things in common. Each of these successful people live by power principles, and these principles dominate their attitudes and daily activities. Unfortunately, in our society today the majority of messages we receive are negative ones, so you have to fight very hard to keep powerful, positive messages as your dominant thought.

For this reason, I have worked with Kelly Morrison for several years, because we have found that combining her powerful, positive messages in music with my messages in my books and speaking engagements, reinforces each power statement. I have put six of these power statements I live by on a beautiful postcard which I would like to give to you. This postcard also has my phone number on it so that any time you are struggling with your own success, you can call me.

I want you to know that from this day forward, you have one person who believes in you, your success, and your destiny. Make a positive step toward your own personal success right now.

Today's the day!

LONG DAYS AND SHORT YEARS

WHEN HE WAS WELL PAST 90 YEARS OF AGE, MY GRANDFATHER SHARED with me a lesson regarding having a sense of urgency about life. He observed that, when we are young, a day can go by in the blink of an eye, but a year seems like forever. We all can remember playing outside on a wonderful summer's day and then observing, as if by magic, somehow the entire day slipped away. But, at the same time, when we are young, the calendar can seem like eternity. The next birthday, Christmas, or the last day of school is impossibly distant.

On the other hand, my grandfather told me that, as we age, a day can drag by while the years roll around before we know it. In our youth, time is judged to be an endless commodity. But, as we reach different milestone birthdays that end with zero, we begin to observe our location along the highway of life.

I, for several years, have participated in an accountability group with several friends I deeply respect. Every other weekend, we have a conference call to discuss commitments we have made and issues that are important in our lives.

One member of our group received a wake-up call from his 12-year-old daughter. As part of a family exercise around the breakfast table one morning, they compiled a list of vacation destinations that they would like to enjoy as a family. When it was all said and done, there were six proposed vacation trips to look forward to. Then, it dawned on my friend that in order to include his oldest daughter, they would need to take one of the trips each summer beginning immediately. Instantly, he realized there was no time to waste, and those precious years that had previously seemed inexhaustible were discovered to be amazingly few.

Think of all of the things you want to do in your life. Examine how far you have come and how much you have left to do. I think you will realize that none of us can afford to waste a year, a month, or even a day. And, as always, *today's the day!*

SUCCESS IS YOUR BABY

THERE WERE TWO WARRING TRIBES IN THE ANDES, ONE THAT LIVED in the lowlands and the other high in the mountains. The mountain people invaded the lowlanders one day, and as part of their plundering of the people, they kidnapped a baby and took the infant with them back up into the mountains.

Although the lowlanders didn't know how to climb the mountain, they sent out their best party of fighting men to bring the baby home. They first tried one method of climbing and then another. They tried one trail and then another. After climbing only a few hundred feet after several days of effort, the lowlander men decided that the cause was lost, and they prepared to return to their village below.

As they were packing their gear for the descent, they saw the baby's mother—with the baby strapped to her back—coming down the mountain that they had been unable to climb. One man greeted her and said, "How did you climb this treacherous mountain when we, the strongest and most able men in the village, couldn't do it?"

She shrugged her shoulders and said, "It wasn't your baby."

Your goal, your dream, your sense of personal destiny, is your baby. Nobody will care for it, rescue it, or work for it like you will. Don't expect it of others. Do expect that kind of care and hard work on your part. And do expect that you will need to pursue your dream with that kind of single-minded focus.

Today's the day!

You Are Here

AS A BLIND PERSON MYSELF, I AM ALWAYS INTRIGUED WITH THE WAY that sighted people get or fail to get from point A to point B. It is fascinating to me that people who can see perfectly spend a great deal of their time being lost.

Recently, I made one of my rare trips to a giant shopping mall. As usual, I was listening to all the conversations going on around me. I discovered that most people spend a great deal of effort during their shopping experience trying to figure out where they are in relation to where they wish they were.

I discovered that throughout the mall, there are a number of maps showing the locations of the various shops and restaurants in the building. These maps are identical at every location throughout the facility with one very critical exception. In each map location, there is one unique piece of information that is the large arrow pointing to a spot on the map with the explanation reading, "You are here."

This points out a vital link in the chain of personal achievement. That is, quite simply, that the single most vital piece of information necessary in order to get where you are going is to know where you are. There are millions of people who want to have a certain bank balance, weigh a certain amount, or achieve any other business or personal goal. These people fantasize about where they want to be, but they have not taken the practical step of determining where they are.

A dream turns into a goal when you get specific. The ancient Chinese proverb says, "A journey of a thousand miles begins with a single step." This is only true if you take that first step in the right direction. That is only possible when you know where you are.

Think about all the things you want in the personal and professional areas of your life. Then take account of where you are today. You may find that you're closer than you think. But, in any event, you will have taken the first step in the right direction, and you will have reduced an ethereal dream into a practical goal that can begin now.

Today's the day!

JUST SAY YES

FOR THE PAST TEN YEARS, I HAVE HAD THE PRIVILEGE OF SPEAKING with thousands of elementary and middle school students. The media would tell us that the state of our youth is alarming. While I would be the first to agree that we have some unique challenges facing us, this generation of young people is very impressive.

When I visit with them, I try to focus on the critical issues they are facing, including drugs, alcohol, destructive relationships, and negative peer pressure. These young people have been pounded with the message "Just Say No." That message was brought to the forefront by former First Lady Nancy Reagan.

While Mrs. Reagan was full of good intentions and probably has brought a positive light to the problem, we must realize that "Just Say No" is not enough. I don't believe there is a kid in America who is unaware of the fact that they are not supposed to take drugs, drink alcohol, etc. The reality is, we have not given them a compelling enough reason to "Just Say No."

As human beings, it is impossible for us to have an emotional, spiritual, or intellectual void. Bad habits, ideas, or concepts can only be replaced with good ones. To go into an inner-city school and tell a group of young people to "Just Say No" is ineffectual. But, when you can somehow equate their dreams, their goals, and their ambitions to being able to stay away from what I call "The Dream Killers", then you have a reason for them to live a positive lifestyle.

The same thing applies to you and me. When we look at our own personal goals or the things we want to achieve out of this life, success generally comes down to replacing bad habits with good ones. Just saying "No" to the bad habit won't do it for you, but if you can fix firmly in your mind the fact that success is dependent upon replacing that bad habit with a good one, you will find that everything is possible.

Say "Yes" to your dream, and the bad habits will take care of themselves. If it can work for students across America, it can work for you and me.

I look forward to your success.

Today's the day!

LESSONS FROM THE TOP
OF THE WORLD

RECENTLY, I HAVE BEEN READING QUITE A BIT ABOUT EXPEDITIONS ON Mount Everest. I am intrigued by the fact that so many people over the years have been driven to climb the tallest mountain on earth and stand on the top of the world.

While studying the expeditions, I have been amazed at how much time, preparation, and energy goes into getting to the mountain with all of the equipment necessary to make the climb and to set up each of the base camps along the route. An expedition is literally years in the planning stage and months in the preparation stage before an attempt can be made on the summit. Then, if the weather is good, the conditions are right, and there are no major accidents, a handful of members from the expedition will have a chance to make it to the top. Out of dozens of climbers who begin the journey, only a few will even have the opportunity on the last day to stand on the top of the world.

On many expeditions, through no fault of their own, all of the climbers return home without even a glimpse of the summit. But at best, people plan for years and work for months to stand for a few moments at the pinnacle.

Our lives and our successes are much the same. No matter what your goal or objective may be, you will spend much more time in its pursuit than you will enjoying your success. For this reason, we must enjoy the journey.

If we examine the way we live our lives, we invest our days pursuing milestones along the route to our personal summit. The milestones we reach are not really a part of our daily life. They are simply points along the way where we measure our progress. Our life is lived in the journey and in the climb toward the top. It is ultimately sad to see individuals pursuing a goal they think they want while they are enduring the personal torture of the pursuit.

If you don't enjoy the journey, there is no destination worth the effort. If you enjoy every step along the way, you will find your moment on the top of the world to be a time of reflection on the wonderful experience you had getting there.

Invest your days in pursuit of a worthwhile summit, but enjoy each day of the climb.

Today's the day!

Keeping On-Course

THERE COMES A TIME IN EVERYONE'S LIFE WHEN YOU BECOME extremely frustrated with your progress toward your goal. There are days when you seem to be making incredible strides, and nothing can stop you. Then, there are those days when your best efforts seem to take you nowhere. That is the time to "stay the course."

Farmers know what it's like to plant a seed and see no progress for weeks at a time. Then, all of a sudden, a plant pops up through the soil, and hope is renewed. Sailors know what it's like to stare at the distant horizon for days on end with no apparent progress. Then, without warning, land is spotted, and the destination looms ahead.

Each of us has this same dilemma to face on a daily basis; however, unlike the farmer who knows the crop will grow because it did last year and the sailor who knows his voyage is at an end because he has been this way before, you and I have no tangible landmarks.

Sometimes the only points we have are our starting point and our destination. We don't get a report in the mail saying, "You are now halfway toward your goal." The wonderful thing about our life goals is that while progress seems to be delayed or non-existent, your efforts are causing things to work behind the scenes that will allow you a quantum leap toward your destiny.

Remember all the times in your life when things were not coming together, but you kept on trying. Then, out of nowhere, you meet the key person, discover the missing element, or find the shortcut you have been looking for. Those magical moments happen only when you "stay the course."

You are closer than you think to success. Just like the farmer who has planted the seed or the sailor who has started his voyage, you will reach your destination if you just keep going. Even though there are days when your goal seems a million miles away. For the farmer, the sailor, or you and me, every day of the journey is critical. They all add up to your success.

Remember, what you do today will bring you one day closer to where you want to be—whether you are able to recognize it at this time or not. Keeping the faith today is the price we pay and, as always, *today's that day!*

The Road to Success

MANY PEOPLE IN OUR SOCIETY ARE LABORING UNDER THE IMPRESSION that they cannot get from where they are to where they want to be. Somehow, they have convinced themselves that the road they are on does not lead to their goals and dreams.

> *For everyone who turns a disadvantage into*
> *an excuse, there is someone else who turns*
> *it into a springboard to greatness.*

I want to assure you that the street in front of your house will take you anywhere you wish to go. You may not now feel that way, but your feelings do not change reality. You may feel that you are on a rougher, more uphill, difficult road than many people. You may feel that you were born the wrong color, gender, national heritage, religion, etc. On the other hand, you may feel that due to a disability or a disadvantaged background, you're on the wrong road. If you look hard enough, you can find someone who was on the same difficult road that you were on who has already reached their ultimate destiny in life. I am not saying that it's easy. I'm simply saying that it's possible.

For everyone who turns a disadvantage into an excuse, there is someone else who turns it into a springboard to greatness. The same tenacity that will help you compensate for that disadvantage will make you mentally tougher than people who have not faced adversity.

You may not appreciate or even like your current situation. I'm not saying that you should. There are many good people who find themselves in very bad circumstances. I do want you to realize that while we don't have choices about what happens to us, we always have choices in what we're going to do about it. Each day we make a decision to either complain about the road we're on or take the road that we have until it intersects with another road and then merges with the highway that leads to everything we want from this life.

Take comfort in knowing that—once you get on the superhighway—you will be able to enjoy it, appreciate it, and maximize the experience because of the struggles and time you have spent on the rough and steep back roads. Today, when you back out of your driveway, realize that that street will take you anywhere you want to go.

Today's the day!

LIVING YOUR DREAMS

THIS IS THE ONE LIFE THAT WE ALL HAVE BEEN GIVEN. THIS IS NOT A practice game. It is the World Series, the Olympics, and the Super Bowl all wrapped up into one. If you don't feel that kind of power and passion about your life, you need to either find something new to do or find a new attitude.

There's a lot of conversation about living your dreams. This is a very important part of success. People spend more time planning their three day weekend than they do planning how they are going to live their lives. Very few people ever take the time to really ask themselves questions and plan where they would like to go. You've heard it said that people don't plan to fail, they simply fail to plan.

This is the one life that we all have been given. This is not a practice game. It is the World Series, the Olympics, and the Super Bowl all wrapped up into one.

So while you are avoiding the pitfall of not planning your life and living out your dreams, it is important to also avoid the pitfall of dreaming your life away. There are many people who get caught up in the pursuit of planning and dreaming and never put anything into practice. We have all met those individuals who are always going to do something, but nothing seems to ever happen. They have learned that dreams cost nothing until we begin to act upon them, so they simply live out their lives in some mythical, futuristic fantasy game.

There is never a convenient time to start on the road to success and begin to live out your dreams. There will always be a handy excuse. Remember the words of General George Patton, "A good plan violently executed today is better than a perfect plan next week." We must all find the delicate balance between spending too much time in dreaming about tomorrow vs. too much time in the realities of today.

If you have a dream or a goal, it was put inside of you for a reason. Each day, you should be progressing toward your goal. You may not know how to get all the way from here to there, but every day gives you the opportunity to learn more, make contacts, and be preparing for your success. Each day will either take you one day closer or one day farther from living out your dreams.

Today's the day!

PRIORITIZE AND ELIMINATE

AS A RESULT OF MY BOOKS, SPEAKING ENGAGEMENTS, AND THESE COL-umns, I hear from a great number of people who are attempting to take charge of their lives.

It has come to my attention that there is a huge gulf between long-range planning and short-term activity. Many people have been to seminars, read books, etc. which have taught them to set their life goals. I would be the first to say this is an extremely valuable pursuit; however, if your short-term or immediate activity does not match up with your long-term goals, you have a huge problem.

Too often, our long-term goals are compartmentalized in our minds into another area that we don't deal with on a daily basis. It's like our Christmas card list: We drag it out once a year, make any changes necessary, send out our cards, and mentally—as well as physically—put the list away for another year.

In a perfect world, someone should be able to follow you throughout your daily activities and, simply by observing the tasks that you perform, determine what your life priorities are. Granted, we all have to walk the dog and change the oil, but at some point in each day, you should be pursuing your life goals.

Recently, I heard from a gentleman who was in one of my audiences in a speaking engagement almost three years ago. He reminded me that after my presentation he got a book and, as I was autographing it for him, he told me that he wanted to move from Canada to California and pursue academic research as his life's work. When this gentleman called me three years later, I happened to remember that brief conversation that he and I had three years previous in the back of an arena.

Unfortunately, three years have come and gone, and he is no closer to his goal than he was before. This is very dangerous, because it reinforces the fact that his life goals are somewhere out in the future and don't have to be dealt with today.

If you have a life's goal or what you consider to be your destiny, you should be taking some action on it every day. There is always something to learn, someone to meet, or some preparation you can take toward that end. Dedicate yourself to making each day an investment in your future.

Today's the day!

WHERE HAVE ALL THE HEROES GONE?

RECENTLY, WE LOST JOE DIMAGGIO, A TRULY GREAT HUMAN BEING. AS I listened to the news reports and retrospectives on his life, he was described as legendary, a great American, a classy individual, a man of honor and integrity, but rarely was the term baseball player used in the lead-ins to these stories.

Joe DiMaggio was a great person who happened to be an extraordinary baseball player. His baseball career gave him a worldwide platform so that we all became aware of his greatness. However, he is known and will be remembered by several generations of people who never watched him play baseball.

His legend transcends the game.

In a recent survey, people who were teenagers during the 1950s, '60s, '70s, '80s, and '90s were asked to list their heroes. Those who were teenagers in the '50s compiled a long and impressive list. Those who represented the decade of the '60s had a shorter but still significant list. Those who were teenagers in the 1970s were able to list very few people who were heroes to them. What is disturbing is that the people who were teenagers in the '80s and '90s were able to identify virtually no heroes.

There may be a number of socio-economic and media factors that account for this decline in heroes, but the bottom line is this: Heroes are not extraordinary people. They are ordinary people who conduct themselves in extraordinary ways.

Those of you who experienced the impact of the motion picture *Saving Private Ryan* will agree that those who came ashore on D-Day to liberate France performed extraordinary feats. It is interesting to realize that these extraordinary feats were accomplished by ordinary young men who were proud to be Americans and found something worth fighting and sacrificing for.

Heroes are not as much rock-and-roll stars and athletes as they are the postman who makes the extra effort to get it done right the first time or the teacher who realizes that the future of our next generation is in her hands as she performs what seems to be her routine, daily task. I hope Joe DiMaggio's life will serve as an example for all of us to find the greatness in the little things we do all day, every day.

During one of the tributes to Joe DiMaggio, there was a video clip from an interview with Joe's teammate, Yogi Berra. Yogi has long been known for his outrageous verbal slips and humorous misstatements. This time Yogi got it right when he said, "I never saw Joe make a mistake either on or off the field. Whatever he was doing, and however it turned out, you always knew Joe DiMaggio did his best." May the same be said of all of us.

Today's the day!

DOING ONE THING WELL

OUR SOCIETY REWARDS PEOPLE HANDSOMELY WHO CAN ONLY DO ONE thing, but can do it well. It's not imperative that the thing they do well be of large significance. News reports are full of the fame, success, and notoriety of Mark McGuire and Tiger Woods. In a global perspective, playing golf or baseball is not terribly important. What matters in this case is how well they do it.

As an author and an interviewer on television, I have had the privilege of speaking with some of the greatest individuals from the worlds of sports, politics, movies, and television. Many of these people have absolutely no skills or talents outside of the one they are known for. You might be shocked to learn that some of the most successful people in our society are incapable of balancing a checkbook, going to the grocery store, or driving a car. They are so good at the things they do that the day-to-day pursuits that invade all of our lives simply don't matter to them.

McDonalds is the most popular and successful food outlet in the world. You can go into McDonalds today and get breakfast, lunch, dinner, salads, healthy foods, junk foods, and any number of other items. But, when they started, McDonalds went for many years only serving one kind of hamburger, French fries, and soft drinks. They perfected their system before they built upon it. I think most people would agree that their success is probably due to their delivery system and their manner of marketing more than their food, itself. The key we can learn from this is that life will reward us when we can do one thing very well and then build on that success to build other successes in the future.

We have all heard about the proverbial "Jack of all trades." These are people who can do a great number of things fairly well, but they're not outstanding at any one thing. While these kinds of people are very handy to have around, they will never be known as super stars in any field, because they lack the focus and the excellence in one specific area.

Work on being known for one thing and doing it exceedingly well. Build your success from there.

Today's the day!

Passion is the Key

ONE OF THE BENEFITS OF BEING PRESIDENT OF THE NARRATIVE TELE-vision Network is that I have the privilege of interviewing many celebrities. These celebrities represent those who are at the very top of their field in sports, politics, television, and movies. These people can teach us many lessons.

My very first interview was with legendary film actress, Katharine Hepburn. After I got over the initial intimidation of talking with her, I began to understand more about her and why she was so successful.

One of the questions I like to ask all celebrities is, "If you had not pursued the career you are now famous for, what do you think you would have done with your life?" Miss Hepburn answered immediately, "It never crossed my mind not to be an actress. I am just fortunate that they pay me—and pay me well—to pursue my passion. If they did not, I would have to find another way to support my habit."

> *If you are not where you want to be along the road to success, you may want to examine not only how hard you are working, but what you are working on.*

This statement gives us a keen insight into the success of Katharine Hepburn, but, more importantly, into what can become our own success. It is a given that in order to reach the top in any field, we are going to have to work long and hard. But, it's interesting to realize that long, hard work doesn't seem like work at all if you are pursuing your passion.

George Burns, another legendary star, once said, "If you enjoy your job, you will never work a day in your life."

If you are not where you want to be along the road to success, you may want to examine not only how hard you are working, but what you are working on. If you don't feel that kind of Katharine Hepburn or George Burns passion, it may be time for you to seek a new direction.

I have heard many motivational speakers say with a bit of a strain in their voice, "You've got to pay the price for success." I don't necessarily believe in that. I believe when you follow your passion, you will enjoy the price of success. If you don't follow your passion, you will pay the price for failure. In the final analysis, what you pursue is more important than how you pursue it.

Today's the day!

THE MAGIC CARD

JUST LAST WEEK WHILE LISTENING TO A RADIO NEWSCAST, I HEARD the most disturbing statistic imaginable. The statistic shocked me so much that I listened to the same newscast a half hour later to be certain that I had heard it right. The radio announcer proclaimed, "Less than 5% of Americans have a library card, and less than 1% use their card with any degree of frequency."

As a blind person, I think back to when I could read a book with my eyes like you are reading this book now. I'm embarrassed to say that at that time in my life, I took reading for granted, and I don't know that I ever read an entire book cover-to-cover. Today, with books-on-tape and a high-speed tape recorder, I read a book every day. This has literally changed my life.

I heard a wise man say once, "You will be the same person five years from today except for the people you meet and the books that you read." At the time, I felt that it was an over-statement of fact. Now I believe, if anything, his words were understated.

Knowledge is the key to anything you want in this life. I've heard it said that if you take all the money in the world and divide it equally among everyone, in a few short years, the money will be back where it is today. In financial terms, the rich get richer and the poor get poorer. It is important to realize, however, that money is not the key. Knowledge is the key. And just as that knowledge allows money to accumulate around people who have attained a certain understanding about money, knowledge will allow you to attract whatever it is that you want in your life.

Virtually anything that you want to know is available for you within a few short miles of where you live at the public library. There is simply no excuse for those people who go through life ignorant of the knowledge it would take for them to reach their goals. You have heard it said, "It's not what you know, but it's who you know." In reality, it is both. Success boils down to both what you know and who you know.

Some of the greatest minds in recorded history are waiting to communicate with you and tell you their secrets of getting anything you want out of this life. Their words, thoughts, and advice are located between the covers of books at your public library. Make a commitment to grow a little each day.

As one of the great cheerleaders of the written word always said, "The more books you read, the taller you grow."

Today's the day!

BEYOND THE SEARCH FOR NORMAL

IN OUR SOCIETY, WE CLAIM TO STRIVE FOR EXCELLENCE, AND CLAIM to honor outstanding achievement. Too often, the reality is that we reward the average. From the time we are small children, we are taught to "fit in" and "don't rock the boat." All of the peer pressure we feel to wear the right clothes, have the right haircut, etc. all teach us to be normal or average instead of outstanding.

If you study excellence historically, you will find that individuals such as Thomas Edison, Benjamin Franklin, and Thomas Jefferson were all eccentric. In no way could they be deemed normal.

We live with the incongruity of the fact that we want extraordinary results but require normal behavior on a day-to-day basis. Sigmund Freud told us that the definition of insanity is to keep doing the same thing while expecting a different result. Many of us would say that we strive for the best and have lofty goals far above the norm. Much more significant to the end result are our daily patterns of performance.

We can look back on an outstanding life of achievement when we can pack every minute of every hour of every day with excellence. An outstanding life is the result of stringing together a long, consistent series of extraordinary days. We spend far too much of our time worrying about what others think of us. In reality, the only opinion that matters is the one that you hold of yourself.

I am quite sure that Edison, Franklin, and Jefferson were regularly ridiculed and derided by people around them. I am equally as sure that it mattered little to them if, indeed, they even realized that they were not "normal."

Never seek an opinion or accept criticism from someone who does not have what you want. Seek out the counsel of mentors and peers who are achievers. Seek their counsel, accept their criticism, and utilize their performance as a measuring stick for your own. Become accountable to someone whose past performance earns your respect. Strive to have extraordinary days while living in a normal world. It doesn't take much to elevate yourself above the crowd.

Today's the day!

The 21st Century Paradox

WE LIVE IN A DAY AND AGE THAT IS FRAUGHT WITH INCONSISTENCY.
Not every advance should be considered to be progress.

As we enter the 21st Century, we are more rushed and have less time than ever before. We are well-fed and poorly nourished. We are well-educated without the benefit of common sense. We have more wealth and less value than generations before us. We have more information at our fingertips but seem to be in a constant state of confusion. We are hurrying faster and getting farther behind. We have millions of options and very few good choices. We have many acquaintances and, virtually, no friends. We have thousands of laws and less and less order. We have instant access and no true communication.

While the world is growing smaller, the gaps between us are expanding. We have extended the quantity of life but not the quality of life. When everything becomes disposable, nothing remains eternal. We have learned the facts of history without learning its lessons. We have learned the secrets of science without learning the responsibility that goes with it.

> *We have more wealth and less value*
> *than generations before us.*

We have learned the mechanics of prospering without learning to live rich lives. We have learned to appear attractive on the outside without learning the art of inner beauty. Free speech has become an excuse for expanding our boundaries to include everything, no matter how much it may diminish our humanity. We have expanded our vocabulary but have very little to say. We have studied the masters without mastering our studies. Our national pastime has become building up celebrities to a heroic proportion and then tearing them down. Our cries for diversity, tolerance, and inclusion often cannot be heard beyond the distances we maintain from each other. We celebrate youth while demanding everyone have experience.

As we stand poised on the brink of a new Millennium, we can see, far in the distance, a new and better tomorrow. Let us always remember that the view we have into the future is only possible because we are standing on the shoulders of the giants who have gone before us. Their lives and words teach us lessons. If we learn from these lessons, the future will be brighter than ever. If we do not learn from these lessons, we will be forced to repeat the struggles of the past.

The key to success in the new Millennium is combining up-to-the-minute, cutting edge technology with principles that have endured from the beginning of time.

Today's the day!

EXPERIENCE LIFE

HOW OFTEN DO YOU HEAR SOMEONE—MAYBE YOURSELF—RESPOND "I've always wanted to do that" after someone else shares about a trip or an experience they have just enjoyed? Think of all the things you have always intended to do. Maybe it's to visit an old friend or classmate. Maybe it's an exotic trip, or maybe it's as simple as going to a museum or a show right in your hometown.

There is a dinner theatre in my hometown that has been performing the same show for decades. Whenever I hear anyone mention that particular production, I hear one of two responses—either "I have been to that" or "I have always wanted to do that."

We seem to have no trouble planning our professional lives. Our work is usually governed by a calendar or a schedule that ensures we get everything done that we intend to do. We have a plan to make a living. The question we need to examine is "Do we have a plan for living our lives?" The reason we plan our work is because we know that a task not scheduled rarely, if ever, gets completed. The same is true in our personal lives. If you don't schedule your vacations, your recreational activities, and your cultural or self-improvement times, they will simply slide to another year and another year and so on.

Think of all the things you have been intending to do for five or ten years or maybe even longer. The very thought of these things signals to us subconsciously that we are not getting all we want out of this life. I would encourage you to get at least as serious about how you live your life as the way you make a living. Start a list of all the things you've ever wanted to do. This list will, quite likely, be very long and will never be completed. You will always be adding things to your "life list."

Schedule a time weekly or at least monthly to review your list, and commit to add one or more of the items from your list to your daily calendar. You will be amazed how the quality of your life will improve and how the time to enjoy the things in this life that are important to you will somehow materialize.

Today's the day!

Life's Shopping List

In today's fast-paced society, we all find ourselves often facing the dilemma of having more tasks to complete than there are hours in the day. People have adopted all manner of tools to assist them in getting as much done as possible. There are fancy calendars, "to-do" lists, priority sheets, computerized day planners, and Palm Pilots, just to mention a few. While all of these may be helpful in their own way as we navigate through the daily struggle between problems and priorities, there is a much more important issue to be addressed: Do you have a system of priorities for your life?

Unfortunately, when we do not have firmly established priorities, we are controlled by people who do.

We would not think of going to the grocery store without a shopping list, lest we come home without some critical item; but few of us have a shopping list for life. We know all of the things we want to get done today or even this week, but we haven't taken the time to think about real long-term priorities.

You can complete every task on your list every day, but if you don't have your priorities in place for your life, you will not succeed in really making a difference in the world. Having life-long priorities will enable you to take control of your daily schedule, because you will be able to judge each activity in light of how it will affect your overall priorities. Unfortunately, when we do not have firmly established priorities, we are controlled by people who do. People will call upon you repeatedly throughout the day for various tasks, missions, contributions, etc. While these may be worthwhile, they are really furthering someone else's life priorities. Until you have your own priorities firmly established, you will fall victim to all manner of detours along the way.

I would highly recommend that—if you do not have your life's shopping list prepared—you squeeze into your daily calendar a specific time to consider all of the possibilities that lie before you. Life offers unlimited menu selections. There are no right or wrong answers. The only mistake is to not make a selection. If you don't know where you're going, how will you ever know when you get there? People who don't make a choice are no better off than people who don't have a choice.

> *If you don't know where you're going, how will you ever know when you get there? People who don't make a choice are no better off than people who don't have a choice.*

All of our lives will be busy, and we will all end up somewhere. Why not dedicate a portion of your daily activities toward reaching your own destiny?

Today's the day!

FISHING LESSONS

RECENTLY, I HAD THE OPPORTUNITY TO SPEND AN AFTERNOON FISH-ing with my father. This is something I highly recommend. He and I spent a lot of time fishing when I was growing up, but now we seem to get out once or twice a year. I find that the fishing is irrelevant. The key is the outing itself and the time we spend together, as well as the lessons I learn.

Fishing is simply an excuse to enjoy an afternoon outdoors with someone you love and respect. Fishing somehow makes it legitimate. If you were to take an afternoon off work, stand at the lakeshore, and talk, you would be considered lazy or unproductive. But if you hold a fishing rod during the process, it makes it all somehow legitimate.

During this last trip, I couldn't help but notice that my father and I were using the same equipment and standing in the same spot, but he consistently caught more fish than I did. I tried not to take this person-ally and tried to take notice of what he was doing different from me. Finally it occurred to me that he was casting out his line many more times than I was. He actually wasn't catching more fish per cast, he was just simply giving the fish more opportunities to be caught.

This is much like our success in life. The most successful among us may not have a higher percentage of success, they simply give themselves more opportunities to succeed. As a totally blind person, I am convinced that I could hit a baseball thrown by the best pitcher in the major league if you would allow me to swing as many times as I wanted to.

When you look at your own career, life, or success, ask yourself: What is the one element that will do more to get me from where I am to where I want to be? Then, perform that critical element as much as possible. There are many sales seminars across the country designed to help those in sales and marketing to improve their closure rate. While these seminars may be beneficial, I would maintain that the easiest way to improve would be to simply make more sales calls.

Let the percentages take care of themselves. Control the things you can control.

If we could ever eliminate the time we spend worrying about things we can't control, and invest that time focusing on the things we can control, we will be miles ahead. Focus on the important things in your day, and take every opportunity you can to go fishing.

Today's the day!

Input and Output

ALL OF US ARE MOVING INTO THE TECHNOLOGY AGE. SOME PEOPLE are embracing technology eagerly while others are being dragged—kicking and screaming—into this brave new world; however, for better or for worse, computers, the Internet, and technology still being developed will all play an integral part in how we all live the rest of our lives.

I find it fascinating that, even with all the miracle developments, ancient principles still govern 21st century technology. One of the leading principles of the computer age is that the information you get out can never be better or more accurate than the information you put in.

We live in a world dominated by the "quick fix" mentality. We are sold on the fact that success and happiness are instantaneous. Just take a pill or win the lottery, etc. All of these messages affect us both consciously and sub-consciously. Our world-view is becoming skewed by our input.

I am in the television business. People in our industry have strange ideas about the messages they send. On one hand, they will tell you that the violence and other explicit material they show really has no impact on people because everyone understands that it is not real. On the other hand, they will sell you 30 seconds of commercial time during the Super Bowl for $2 million because they will convince you that you will sell enough corn chips or snow tires in just 30 seconds to offset the cost of the ad. You can't have it both ways.

Just like the computer, your mind is subject to what goes into it. Unlike the computer, you can control your own input.

Don't be fooled by the "quick fix" mentality of the media. Success and happiness are not simply a matter of drinking the right beverage or wearing the appropriate fragrance. Success and happiness, instead, are a matter of deciding what you want to give and receive out of this life—and then controlling the messages that you input into your mind in order to reach your destiny.

The most cutting-edge computer may have amazing power and speed, but it is still subject to the fact that that you reap what you sow. Control your input, and your output will take care of itself.

Today's the day!

The Gift of Learning

My most popular book, *The Ultimate Gift,* has been released internationally. Each time I write a book or even one of these weekly columns, I am struck by the irony of the situation. As a blind person, myself, I realize that this column you are reading has been written by someone who can't read it—or at least not in the way you do.

The wisdom of the ages, the answer to any questions, the ability to be informed, entertained, and educated, is as close as your nearest bookstore or library.

When I could read with my eyes—just as you are doing at this moment—I don't know that I ever read an entire book cover to cover. This is not something of which I am particularly proud; however, it is the truth. I had not yet come to understand The Gift of Learning. Now, as a totally blind person I read a book every day, thanks to the National Library for the Blind which provides books on tape and a high-speed tape recorder. Having read 365 books a year for the last 12 years, I have experienced a myriad of changes in my life and in my world.

The wisdom of the ages, the answer to any questions, the ability to be informed, entertained, and educated, is as close as your nearest bookstore or library. The greatest men and women of all times are available via books to share with you their greatest secrets.

Start a list of all the books you want to read. Keep updating the list constantly. When someone tells you about something they have read or you hear about a new book in the media, make a note of it. Your lifelong reading list will become a constant companion. You will always be adding new titles and marking off ones you have completed.

When I began to read consistently, I started to grow in every way. Prior to becoming a reader, the idea of authoring multiple books or even writing this weekly column seemed absurd. You will never know the hidden strength inside of you or the hidden treasures within books until you make an effort to become a reader.

In the beginning, like any new habit, it will seem awkward and difficult. After several weeks or months, you will find yourself quite anxious to get back to your reading each day. I hope you will enjoy my book and movie, *The Ultimate Gift*, and many other titles throughout the rest of your life. Every day is an opportunity to grow and learn.

Today's the day!

JUST SAY NO

MANY OF US RUSH THROUGH OUR LIVES AT A FRANTIC PACE AND, AT the end of the day, we lament the fact that we did not do enough. In reality, it is not the fact that we don't get enough done, but that, instead, we try to do too much.

There is a major difference between being busy all day and actually accomplishing meaningful tasks. In order to determine whether a task is meaningful, one must know what he or she is trying to accomplish. While this seems over-simplistic, it is the failure trap that catches more people than anything else on a day-to-day basis. When we're not sure where we're going, any movement seems productive. There's a huge difference between activity and productivity.

Each morning, you must look at your "to do" list and ask yourself, "Which of these things is really getting me closer to my ultimate objective?" And, as you look at each of the items on your list, it is also good to ask yourself the question—as you contemplate each activity—"What happens if I don't do this?"

Oftentimes, the act of being busy simply occupies our time, effort, and energy and takes our focus away from where we really should be. Performing with excellence while accomplishing the wrong task can, indeed, be worse than doing nothing at all, because it creates habits and patterns that are very hard to break.

The key to success is learning to say "Yes" to the right things. This becomes easy when you learn how to say "No" to the wrong things. The wrong things are not necessarily in and of themselves bad things; they are simply not leading to your personal destiny. The wrong thing or activity for you might very well be the right thing for someone else, because their destination lies in a totally different area.

The Cheshire cat in *Alice in Wonderland* leaves us with a fabulous message. "If you don't know where you're going, it really doesn't matter which road you take."

Examine your personal and career goals in light of how you spend your time. Could a total stranger determine your goals by simply watching your daily activities? Make sure that each day is an investment in your future and not simply another rat race experience on the same old treadmill.

Today's the day!

CHICKEN OR BEEF?

AS A FORMER NATIONAL CHAMPION OLYMPIC WEIGHTLIFTER, ONE OF my prized possessions is my gold medal. It is a very special memento to me, which I display in my office. Recently, I was traveling on an airplane, and I met a unique gentleman seated next to me. If they ever add an Olympic event called the Marathon Bad Attitude, this gentleman will have a gold medal, too.

Shortly after introducing myself, he told me he didn't like the airline we were flying on, the seats, the aisles, or our flight attendant. He went on to inform me he didn't like the city we were in, the airport we were connecting through, or our final destination. I don't think he liked me either, but we didn't get that far into the conversation.

There are a few people who make the right decisions, and there are a few people who make the wrong decisions, but the vast majority of people really never make a decision at all. They simply complain about the results.

After we took off, our flight attendant told us that we would have a choice of chicken or beef for our dinner. I told her I would enjoy the chicken dinner, and my "Olympian seat mate" told her he didn't care which one he got. She informed him that he was a first class passenger on this airline and it was her job to make him happy, and they had plenty of both the chicken and the beef, so she would be delighted to bring him whichever one he would prefer. He informed her once again, "It really doesn't matter—just bring me something."

A few moments later she returned with my chicken dinner, and gave him the beef dinner. For the next 41 minutes of this flight (I actually timed it on my Braille watch), he told me everything you can imagine, and some things you could not imagine, that was wrong with his beef dinner, and why he wished he had the chicken dinner. I realized that this is the way most people live their lives. There are a few people who make the right decisions, and there are a few people who make the wrong decisions, but the vast majority of people really never make a decision at all. They simply complain about the results. These are people who spend more time planning their three-day weekend than they do planning the rest of their lives.

This life we are living right now is not a practice game. It is the Super Bowl and the World Series and the Olympics all rolled up into one. If you do not feel that way about your life and what you do, you need to do something different or get a new attitude about the things you do now. Your destiny awaits.

Today's the day!

DO IT NOW

AS WE SEEK SUCCESS IN OUR PERSONAL AND PROFESSIONAL LIVES, IT IS critical that we identify and understand our enemy. Failure is not the enemy of success. Procrastination is the enemy of success. More people fall short of their goal not because their best efforts were lacking, but they fall short because they never started.

My good friend and colleague, Dr. Robert Schuller, often says, "Starting is halfway done." For years, I thought this was false because I thought starting was just the beginning and couldn't be close to halfway done. The ensuing years and experiences have taught me that if Dr. Schuller's words are less than accurate, it is because starting is much more than halfway done.

Failure is not the enemy of success.
Procrastination is the enemy of success.

Too often, we feel that success is fragile, and our initial efforts will not be sufficient to build upon; therefore, we never start. If perfection is your goal, you are doomed to fail. There is never a perfect time to begin a task, quest, or journey. If you're waiting for all the lights to be green, the weather to be perfect, and every condition to be favorable, you will never get off the launching pad.

If you have a goal, a dream, or an objective you would like to pursue in your life, probably the best single piece of advice I could give you is to get started. Sometimes, people begin a task and do not initially reach their objective, but I can promise you no one reaches their objective without starting. The one thing that every great success has in common is that someone determined their best efforts were good enough, and they did something today.

If you have a passion inside of you to reach some future goal, you should be doing something to further your cause today. Maybe you're studying, maybe you're meeting people, or maybe you're beginning the steps that will take you from here to there; but unless there is a specific focused point that you have determined is best for your launch, you need to do something today. And even if your launch is weeks, months, or even years in the future, you need to be making preparations and laying the ground work.

Other than fine wine, few things in life are improved with age. If you are going to do it, do it now. If you're not going to do it, find something you are going to do and do it now.

Today's the day!

DEFINING YOURSELF

ALL OF US SPEND FAR TOO MUCH TIME, EFFORT, AND ENERGY WORRYing about what other people think about us. We would spend far less time worrying about what other people think about us if we realized how seldom they do. In the final analysis, the only opinion about us that matters is the opinion we hold of ourselves. This involves a level of self-evaluation and honesty that few people achieve.

One of the great writers of all time, William Shakespeare, wrote, "To thine own self be true." This is very simple but not very easy. In order for us to fully understand who we are, we first have to be clear on who we are not. The great sculptor, Michelangelo, when asked how he was able to take a block of granite and turn it into a beautiful woman, replied, "You simply find a block of granite and remove everything that is not a beautiful woman." All of us have talents and abilities that, if fully exploited, would make us successful. Unfortunately, we too often perform outside of our level of talent and expertise.

One of the advantages I find in being blind is that there are so many things I cannot do. This leaves a handful of things I can do where I can focus my efforts and energy. This narrow focus has brought me a high degree of success, happiness, and satisfaction. If you have all five senses, you will have to take on the added task of focusing your energy in certain areas while eliminating others where you could perform if you wanted to.

Remember, Michael Jordan was arguably the best basketball player that has ever played the game; but when he decided to play baseball, he was barely a mediocre Minor League player. Playing in the Minor Leagues is great if that's all you can do. I would argue that each of us has Major League talent and ability if we will simply play the right game and not play the wrong ones.

Everyone you can think of who has ever achieved greatness has focused their talent in a narrow range. Anyone attempting to be great at everything is destined, at best, to be average at a lot of things and great at nothing. Try observing yourself objectively as if you were evaluating an employee. Give yourself an annual review. Determine what you do well and where you perform at only an average level. Begin to work on eliminating the average until you only deal with the things you do well. The more specialized you become as you focus on your greatness, the more you will succeed.

As you go through your day today, determine to undergo an honest self-evaluation. Move toward your area of greatness, and away from everything else.

Today's the day!

INTENSITY VS. CREATIVITY

THERE ARE ONLY TWO WAYS TO OVERCOME ANY CHALLENGE. YOU either must employ intensity or creativity. There are some situations that require creativity. An old problem must be looked at in a new way, or a new solution must be developed toward existing circumstances. On the other hand, there are problems and challenges that will only respond to prolonged and sustained intensity. You must simply beat on the door repeatedly until it opens or caves in.

The artistry in human endeavor comes into play when we determine whether we are going to utilize intensity or creativity. The two traits are invaluable if you are going to be successful, but they are never interchangeable. Too often, there are people who want to use creativity when a situation requires intensity. They are looking for "get rich quick," "magic pill," or "short cut" solutions to situations that require good old fashioned work and intensity.

Whether you want to get in shape, become financially independent, or get a post graduate degree, there is a lot of marathon-like work involved. People who are looking for microwave solutions to crock pot challenges never succeed. The tortoise and the hare taught us all this when we were in preschool. Unfortunately, life has to remind us from time to time.

On the other hand, there are situations that require creativity and will simply not respond to intensity. There are uninformed people who mistakenly find misguided virtue in working hard instead of working smart. They would rather repeatedly beat their head against an immovable wall instead of going around the wall, climbing over it, or finding the passage that leads to the other side.

If you keep doing the same thing you've always done, you're going to achieve the same result. If you keep doing the same thing with more intensity, you will likely achieve more of the same result. I am sure you have met people in your personal and professional lives who are always looking for the easy way to do everything. On the other hand, I'm sure you know people who seem to want to do everything the hard way. The next time you are presented with an immediate challenge, before you leap in, think for a minute about whether this is a situation that will best respond to creativity or intensity. Once you have determined how you are going to proceed, obstacles seem to become far less daunting.

As you go through your day today, don't forget to employ both of the tools at your disposal—intensity and creativity.

Today's the day!

The Power Zone

In order to maximize your potential, you must understand that power is not universal and skills are not transferable. Just because you can do one thing well does not mean you can do anything else at the same level.

As a former National Champion Olympic weightlifter, I was among the strongest people in the world. Within a very narrow range of motion, I could lift more weight than three or four normal men. This range of motion was a zone approximately one inch wide that ran from the floor to above my head. When I lifted the weight within this power zone where I had trained my strength and focused my skill, I was very successful. If I got out of this power zone by lifting the weight too close to my body or too far out in front of me, my strength fell off geometrically.

Most professional golfers can drive a golf ball close to 300 yards or more; however, if you move the golf ball a matter of inches away from them or closer to them, it will disrupt their swing and they will be out of their power zone. The result will be a dramatically shorter and less accurate golf shot.

Every major league pitcher knows every batter he will be facing. A batter may be a home run threat if the pitch is high and outside, but he will be unable to hit the ball or will ground to the short stop if you pitch him low and inside. Competition is a microcosm of life. There is a winner, a loser, and a clearly established way to keep score; therefore, many life lessons can be derived from sports.

In your career and in mine, we have our own power zones. This zone is represented by the activities where we maximize our effectiveness and our efficiency. Within this power zone, we are proficient and profitable. Outside of this power zone, our performance falls off. If you don't know the exact boundaries of your power zone, you need to ask those around you who know you best and who will be totally honest with you. Identifying and staying within your power zone is the key to everything you want to achieve in your life both personally and professionally.

As you go through your day today, find your power zone and stay in it.

Today's the day!

Magic in the Details

Since losing my sight and getting a new vision for my life, many exciting things have happened to me. I have the privilege of owning and operating a television network; I get to travel and speak at arena and corporate events across the country; I have written a number of books; and, each week, I have the privilege of communicating with people like you around the world via this column in magazines, newspapers, and online publications.

Recently, another exciting thing is unfolding. Just like any other new development, it brings opportunities, privileges, and lessons. One of my novels, *The Ultimate Gift*, is being made into a major motion picture starring James Garner, Lee Meriwether, and Brian Dennehy. I just spent a week on the movie set and actually got to play a small part, myself, in the upcoming film.

When you go to a movie theatre, get your popcorn, and settle into a comfortable seat for two hours of escape and entertainment, it is impossible to think about the time, effort, and energy that literally hundreds of people put into that experience. While on the set, and while doing my scene, I met scores of people. Some were performing tasks you would expect, and others were doing things that are still a mystery to me. However, the lesson came when I realized that all of these people work together for several hours to put together a scene so that the actors and director can come together and, hopefully, shoot a minute or two of film that might make it into a movie. If just one person fails to do their job, the whole thing falls apart and everyone has to start over. This creates a collective sense of urgency for each person to do their job well and not let down the team.

After I left the movie set and came back to the real world, I realized that this same principle can apply to you and me in our daily lives. It takes a whole team of people to excel, and it only takes one person letting down for one minute to make the whole operation look bad.

No matter how well you do your job, if the person who answers your phone, vacuums your carpet, distributes your mail, services your customer, etc. has a bad day or even a bad moment, you and your whole team are judged by your weakest link. If, instead, you appreciate everyone's role and encourage them to do their best at all times for the collective good just like in the movies you can provide a great experience for the people with which you deal; and every once in a while, you can create magic.

As you go through your day today, don't try to get one thing a lot better. Strive to get a lot of things a little better.

Today's the day!

THE TIME OF YOUR LIFE

I REMEMBER THE FIRST TIME I SPOKE WITH SOMEONE WHO WAS OVER 100 years old. As a young person at that time, it was hard for me to conceive of a century of life. When I asked this centenarian what they found most surprising after living 100 years, the response amazed me then as it does now. "I am most surprised about how fast the time flew by."

Each day, week, month, and year, time seems to compress. We have more distractions competing for our precious minutes each day; therefore, it is more important than ever that we take control of the time of our lives.

I am in a bi-monthly accountability group with two other individuals who share my philosophies on life and how we should live it. Every other week, we discuss our goals and priorities. This has been going on for years and has been a very meaningful part of my schedule.

One of the other people in the group told me of an experience in his home that put the time crunch into perspective. The oldest of his three children had her thirteenth birthday, therefore officially reaching that stage of life known as the teenage years. At this young lady's thirteenth birthday party, their family had a discussion that shifted to what they should do on their vacation. The thirteen-year-old, along with the other two children, wrote down several vacation destinations they wanted to experience as a family.

My friend was shocked to learn that, while there were almost 20 potential family vacations that everyone wanted to experience, he had only five summers left before his daughter would go off to college. While this was a sobering realization for their family, it also got them energized to go, do, and experience much more of life while they are still together as a family unit.

Think of all the things you want to do in your life. Invest some time, effort, and energy to write them down. Now, mentally spread those activities over what you project to be the rest of your life. You will discover a sense of urgency about accomplishing these priorities, and you will look at each day as an opportunity to take control of the time of your life.

Today's the day!

SPEED VS. PROGRESS

FOR SOME PEOPLE, DRIVING AN AUTOMOBILE CAN BE A RELAXING experience giving them the opportunity to catch up on the news, listen to enjoyable music, or invest their time hearing audio books or instructional recordings. For other people, driving in traffic is a frantic, hectic procedure that borders on becoming a hostile, full-contact sport. I am sure you have observed both driving behaviors during your daily commute. Sometimes, these two different driving styles or reflections of lifestyles come into a clear focus offering an obvious comparison.

Imagine, if you will, our calm, relaxed driver enjoying beautiful music or an informative, interesting audio book, while slowly approaching a red light. Our calm driver will safely and efficiently drift to an easy, undisturbing complete stop at the traffic light. Meanwhile, our hectic, overstressed fellow motorist will madly accelerate toward the red light and, at the very last instant, slam on the brakes, squealing to a jolting, skidding, abrupt halt.

During the red light, our calm, relaxed, effective driver will continue to enjoy the entertaining music or audio book while looking around at the delightful sights of a beautiful day. Meanwhile, our hectic, overstressed commuter friend will rev the engine, pound on the steering wheel with teeth gritted, waiting for the fraction of an instant when the light changes. All other sensation has stopped while waiting for the light to turn green.

As the light turns green, our calm, relaxed, efficient driver will safely and prudently accelerate into the traffic, moving forward toward a meaningful destination. Meanwhile, our hectic, frantic, unproductive commuter will instantly honk the horn as the light turns green so that anyone who may have paused a fraction of an instant knows that they are immediately to move. After blaring the horn, this driver will jam down the accelerator, at which point the tires will squeal matching the sight, sound, and smell of the stopping skid as the car rockets forward. Our unproductive driver will barrel past our calm, relaxed driver, weave in and out of traffic, and advance like a speeding bullet toward the next intersection.

> *Don't ever confuse activity with productivity, and*
> *remember that speed is not necessarily progress.*

As the next light turns red, this overstressed driver will, once again, slide to an abrupt bone-jarring stop, pounding on the steering wheel in frustration after having missed still another traffic light. As the frustration continues to build and unproductivity grows, our productive and efficient driver will glide to a stop right next to the unproductive, steering-wheel pounding fellow commuter who is preparing to have some kind of traffic-induced seizure.

You may have noticed that two people can have similar vehicles, exactly the same course and destination, and arrive at the same time with completely different focus and results. Don't ever confuse activity with productivity, and remember that speed is not necessarily progress.

As you go through your day today, look for ways to be productive and avoid frantic, hectic speed that is often disguised as true and lasting progress.

Today's the day!

AFTERWORD

AT THE END OF EVERY *WINNERS' WISDOM* COLUMN THAT HAS APPEARED in hundreds of newspapers, magazines, and online publications for many years, my thoughts and ideas end with one simple phrase. "Today's the Day!"

Sometimes, it's hard to know what success is, where it is, or who it is, but the "when" of success is easy to identify because it's today. Yesterday is a canceled check that holds no value. Tomorrow is a promissory note that may or may not prove to have worth, but today is cash. We must spend it well, and use it wisely.

If you have a goal, a quest, or a destination in mind for your life, you will spend many days traveling and only one day arriving, but every day matters. If you wait 'til tomorrow, you will be one day further from your goal. Whatever you achieve or generate today must be a part of your destiny because you traded one day of your life to get it.

You can earn money or lose it. You can build a building, tear it down, and build another, but today can never be replaced. The wisdom in these pages will be nothing more than a useless theory until you apply it in your own life, and to that end, ***today is, indeed, the day.***

JIM STOVALL
2014

ABOUT JIM STOVALL

Jim Stovall is the president of the Emmy Award-winning Narrative Television Network. He is the author of the bestselling book, *The Ultimate Gift,* which is now a major motion picture starring James Garner and Abigail Breslin. He has authored 25 other books that have been translated into over 20 languages.

For additional information about Napoleon Hill products, please contact the following locations:

Napoleon Hill World Learning Center
Purdue University Calumet
2300 173rd Street
Hammond, IN 46323-2094
Judith Williamson, Director
Uriel "Chino" Martinez, Assistant/Graphic Designer
Telephone: 219-989-3173 or 219-989-3166
email: nhf@purduecal.edu

Napoleon Hill Foundation
University of Virginia–Wise
College Relations
Apt. C 1 College Avenue
Wise, VA 24293
Don Green, Executive Director
Annedia Sturgill, Executive Assistant
Telephone: 276-328-6700
email: napoleonhill@uvawise.edu
Website: www.naphill.org